6/9/16

SELECTED SPEECHES
VOLUME 4

GOD BLESS!

KWAME NKRUMAH

Compiled by Samuel Obeng

FROM: DADDY PIERRE ADULLEY EZOUA

TO: JASON EZOUA-NYAMEKE ADULLEY

AFRAM PUBLICATIONS (GHANA) LTD.

WILLIAMS COLLEGE

WILLIAMSTOWN, MA

Published by:

Afram Publications (Ghana) Ltd.,
P. O. Box M. 18,
Accra, Ghana

First Published 1997

ISBN 9964 70 204 3

Typeset by Damana Graphics

Printed by Sakoa Press,

FOREWORD

In the very first Volume of these Works published in 1973 it was suggested that, that Dr. Kwame Nkrumah, "a man who was (in his lifetime) so maligned, condemned and rejected by his own people should at his death be praised and loved so much and be finally accepted by his own people again, appears to testify to Nkrumah's charisma." This proposition has since it was made assumed greater significance in the light of later developments.

Since Dr. Kwame Nkrumah's death the Nkrumah factor has been very forcefully projected in politics and even in the daily lives of the people of Ghana and Africa. Nkrumah's influence has dominated the conduct of the majority of political parties in Ghana. These parties have all laid claim to descent from Dr. Kwame Nkrumah's Convention People's Party and to the Nkrumahist ideology.

Over the period Dr. Nkrumah's statute which was "brutalised" and shoved into obscurity has been re-created and displayed at the Mausoleum built for him in Accra. Furthermore his mortal remains have been transferred from his lowly Nkroful hometown and re-interred at this Mausoleum built and named after him at the very grounds in Accra where he proclaimed independence status for the then Gold Coast forty years ago.

Dr. Nkrumah was concerned with the unity and development of the whole of Ghana. He was concerned with the total welfare of its citizens; his was a vision of a welfare society where all in Ghana would enjoy a reasonably improved standard of life, hence his emphasis on the provision of social amenities like, health, and education. By this strategy he hoped to achieve accelerated economic development.

Nkrumah was passionately committed to the total liberation of the African continent and its eventual unity.

These concerns for domestic and international harmony and development are reflected in all his speeches, short and long, delivered at home and at numerous international fora. Some of the issues he addressed have over the years been resolved; but others like stability in Africa, improved social facilities for Ghana are still relevant.

iii

When one talks of the indestructibility of the tongue it is in reference to the spoken word. In Dr. Kwame Nkrumah's speeches one finds this clearly illustrated. Hardly a national celebration passes without a reminder of Kwame's famous old Polo Grounds Speech declaring Ghana's Independence.

These volume of "Selected Speeches of Dr. Kwame Nkrumah" comes in the fortieth year of Ghana's Independence. It is hoped that the work will urge Ghanaians and friends of Ghana to push ahead with the principles and ideals which some fifty years and more ago inspired the struggle to build Ghana into a "middle level economy."

Accra
August, 1997

William Yaw Eduful
(Publicity Director)
Publicity Secretariate,
Flagstaff House, Accra.

PREFACE

Osagyefo Dr. Kwame Nkrumah had always been in the vanguard of what he himself called "The African Revolution." He had not only been at the centre of its political action, but had also articulated its ideology.

After Dr. Nkrumah's Government was overthrown by a military coup d' etat, on February 24, 1966, he was so much maligned, condemned and rejected by his own people that his books, speeches and pictures that could be reached were publicly burnt.

One afternoon in August, 1971 when I heard a news broadcast on Ghana Broadcasting Corporation Radio that an Act 380 of 28th August, 1971, had banned the use of any slogan by word or shiboleth, photograph, or policy document intended to revive the Convention People's Party (CPP) or its leader or chairman Dr. Kwame Nkrumah, I decided to gather the speeches from those who had them.

I wrote to the Government of the National Redemption Council when the obnoxious Act 380 of August, 1971 was repealed by NRCD 21 of 9th February, 1972, and was given a written permission to compile and publish the Speeches of Kwame Nkrumah.

Kwame Nkrumah's speeches, most of which are being presented together to the world in these volumes, still glow with the force of his personality, his conviction in the face of powerful opposition, his originality, his vision as well as his impatience when his expectations seemed delaying.

Nkrumah did not live to see all his dreams realised, but in his speeches and writings, he has left for posterity ideas which should inspire Africans and Black people everywhere.

It is my hope that readers of these volumes and future generations will derive from these pages the inspiration to fight to uproot the remnants of colonialism from the society.

Samuel Obeng
Compiler

Kumasi,
August, 1997

Dedicated to
politicians and Ex-servicemen
and Brothers and Sisters in the Diaspora
who laid down their lives
to make Ghana's Independence possible

"Truth forever on the scaffold,
Wrong forever on the throne
Yet that scaffold sways the future,
And, behind the dim unknown,
Standeth God within the shadow,
Keeping watch above his own."

—James Russel Lowell

CONTENTS

THE VISIT OF CHOU EN-LAI

STATE DINNER IN HONOUR OF
THE PREMIER OF THE STATE COUNCIL OF
THE PEOPLE'S REPUBLIC OF CHINA

January 13, 1964

PREMIER CHOU EN-LAI, OUR FRIENDS FROM CHINA,
YOUR EXCELLENCIES,

J am happy to welcome you Premier Chou En-Lai and your party to our country, and I do so on my own behalf and on behalf of the people of Ghana. I am glad that it has been possible for you to accept our invitation to visit us.

I still retain the most vivid recollections of my extremely interesting and enjoyable visit to your great country in 1961. Although your visit would be brief, you can be assured that during your stay here you will enjoy our traditional Ghanaian hospitality and experience the warm friendship which all Ghanaians have for all the Chinese people.

Here in Ghana, we admire the great strides made by the People's Republic of China, since the Revolution, under the dynamic leadership of Chairman Mao Tse Tung, Poet, Philosopher, Soldier, and Statesman. You yourself Premier Chou En-Lai have been a foremost stalwart nationalist and freedom fighter in the struggle for the improvement of living conditions of your people.

During your visit, you will see something of the efforts we are making to reconstruct Ghana after years of colonial rule and despoilation. And here, I would like to express the sincere gratitude of the Government and people of Ghana for the assistance which we have received from the Government of the People's Republic of China in helping us in our industrial and agricultural development.

We believe that in countries impoverished by colonial

exploitation, the surest road to the welfare and happiness of all the people lies in socialism. We believe that the condition of the welfare of each should be the condition for the welfare and development of all.

Premier Chou-En-Lai, we are particularly happy to see you in our midst at a time when our nation is on the verge of taking a decisive step forward in its determination to build and sustain a socialist society.

This, your first visit to Africa, is an occasion of great significance. You have come as a distinguished representative of a dynamic and energetic people - nearly 650 million people - who have been welded together into a strong nation, united and progressive. Surely, this example should inspire us in Africa and leave no doubt in our minds that a continental union Government of Africa is not only possible but a reality. We are unalterably convinced that only a continental Government of Africa can put an end to Africa's want and misery. A united Africa will be a strong link in the chain of Afro-Asian anti-imperialist solidarity. We shall speak with one voice and fight together to make the world safe for mankind.

Premier Chou En-Lai, in this connection, I must express our feeling of regret and disappointment in that your great country remains outside the United Nations Organisation. The Government of Ghana shall continue to support the restoration of the legitimate rights of the Chinese people in the United Nations.

Please, take note that our struggle against colonialism and imperialism is part of the struggle for world peace. For there can be no lasting peace until imperialism, colonialism and neo-colonialism are wiped out completely from the face of the earth. And we too take note that in this struggle, China can make a great contribution towards that peace which alone can sustain our civilisation. It is owing to our unshakable belief in the necessity for world peace that we adhere so steadfastly to the five principles of co-existence established in Bandung, namely, respect for each other's territorial integrity and sovereignty, non-aggression, non-interference in each other's internal affairs, equality and mutual benefit and co-existence.

If only the imperialists and neo-colonialists would accept and abide by these principles, I am sure that world peace would be established and preserved for all time. We would then really live in a world without war.

Esteemed Premier Chou-En-Lai, let me once again extend to you and your party a very warm welcome to Ghana. I hope that you will find your stay enjoyable and pleasant.

And now Your Excellencies, Dear Friends, I ask you to rise with me and drink a toast - a toast to the leaders and people of China, to Chairman Mao Tse Tung and also to you Premier Chou En-lai for the part you played in your country's revolution.

Long Live Sino-Ghana friendship!

Long Live African Unity!

Long Live Peace and Friendship among the nations.

3

2

CHOU EN-LAI IN GHANA

DINNER HELD IN HONOUR OF OSAGYEFO
BY PREMIER CHOU EN-LAI

The Castle
January 15, 1964

PREMIER CHOU EN-LAI, DEAR FRIENDS,

J want to say how glad we have been to welcome you and members of your party to Ghana. Although your visit has been short we hope that you have enjoyed your stay, and that you will return for a longer visit soon - a visit that, I hope will take place in the bosom of a united Africa.

It was a great pleasure for us to have had you among us.

Your visit has given us the opportunity to exchange views on many important matters of mutual interest. I am sure that our talks will be of benefit not only to Ghana and China and to the furtherance of Afro-Asian solidarity, but that they will also contribute greatly towards international progress and world peace.

As an emerging and developing country, we recognise how vital it is for us to take advantage of the experience and assistance which, under the dynamic leadership of Chairman Mao Tse Tung, yourself, Marshall Chen Yi and other leaders of the Chinese Revolution, in spite of great odds, have been able to establish a great nation. My friends, in the world of to-day, there can never be two Chinas.

The example of China's determination, organisation, discipline and unity cannot be lost on Africa at this time. Indeed, it inspires us in Africa to take concrete steps within the territories and states of Africa towards the political unification of our Continent.

We have learnt with interest, the methods by which the people of China have mobilised their resources for the reconstruction of their country and the improvement of their living conditions.

4

We are particularly impressed by the ways and means used by China to accumulate funds, as for example increasing state revenue through the development of production; the all-out practice of thrift and economy that exists, and the way she has succeeded in keeping low the production and distribution costs and commodities.

We note too, that China's investment funds come chiefly from state enterprises which are owned and managed by the state on behalf of the people and that a part of the total income earned by these enterprises is handed over to the Government by the workers as profits and taxes. The peasants also, after deducting from their gross income through enough for their personal living expenses and reserves for expansion, contribute a portion of their earnings to the Government.

I am sure that we can learn much from China to help us in our plans for the development of Ghana. In this respect, we have been learning not only from the West, but also from the East.

We hope that you will carry back with you happy memories of your stay in Ghana. Please convey to Chairman Mao Tse Tung, the President and other leaders of your great country, and to the people of China, our fraternal and affectionate greetings.

And now, may I ask you to rise with me and drink a toast to Premier Chou En-Lai, and his party, and to the success and happiness of the Government and people of China.

Long Live Sino-Ghana Friendship!

Long Live Peace, Friendship and Understanding throughout the world!

JOINT GHANA-CHINA COMMUNIQUE

At the invitation of the President of the Republic of Ghana, Osagyefo Dr. Kwame Nkrumah, the Premier of the State Council of the People's Republic of Ghana, Chou En-Lai, paid a friendly return visit to Ghana from January 11 to 16, 1964. Premier Chou En-Lai was accompanied by Marshal Chen Yi, Vice-Premier of the State Council and Minister of Foreign Affairs, together with other officials of the People's Republic of China.

During his stay in Ghana, Premier Chou En-Lai and his entourage made a tour of interesting places in Accra, including Tema Harbour and the industrial centres in the vicinity. The distinguished guests were cordially received everywhere and had an opportunity to learn personally the feelings of warm friendship which the Ghanaian people have for the Chinese people and their representatives. The Premier was impressed by developments in Ghana and expressed great appreciation under the leadership of President Nkrumah, in safeguarding national independence and developing the national economy. Premier Chou En-Lai admired the role of Ghana and its leader in the vanguard of the National Liberation Movement in Africa, in promoting African solidarity and in defending world peace.

In the course of the visit, the Premier of the State Council of the People's Republic of China had meetings and conversations with Osagyefo Dr. Kwame Nkrumah, President of the Republic of Ghana. Taking part in these talks on the Ghanaian side were Kojo Botsio, Minister of Foreign Affairs, E. K. Bensah, Minister of Communications and Works and Chief of State Protocol, S. A. Dzirasa, Deputy Minister of Foreign Affairs, E. K. Okoh, Secretary to the Cabinet, M. F. Dei-Anang, Ambassador (Special Duties), F. S. Arkhurst, Principal Secretary, Ministry of Foreign Affairs, K. B. Asante, Principal Secretary, African Affairs Secretariat, Joe Fio Meyer, Ghana Ambassador-designate to the People's Republic of China, W. Y. Eduful, Director Publicity Secretariat, J. B. Wilmot, Acting Director, Eastern Department, Ministry of Foreign Affairs.

On the Chinese side were Marshal Chen Yi, Vice Premier of the State Council and Minister of Foreign Affairs, Kung Yuan, Deputy Director of Office in charge of Foreign Affairs, State Council, Huang Chen, Vice Minister of Foreign Affairs, Tung Hsiao-peng, Chief of the Secretariat of Premier of the State Council, Chiao Kuan-Hua, Assistant Minister of Foreign Affairs, Huang Hua, Chinese Ambassador to Ghana, Wang Yu-tien, Director of the West Asian and African Department, Ministry of Foreign Affairs.

The conversations between the leaders of the Republic of Ghana and the People's Republic of China were held in an atmosphere of cordial friendship and complete mutual understanding and were characterised by the reciprocal desire to discuss frankly the major international problems as well as questions pertaining to Sino-Ghanaian relations.

The exchanges of opinion revealed a community of views on such problems as imperialism, colonialism and neo-colonialism, general disarmament, the complete prohibition of nuclear weapons, the settlement of international issues through peaceful negotiations and the strengthening of Afro-Asian peoples' solidarity against imperialism.

The two parties noted that the greatest danger facing mankind at this time emanated from imperialism, colonialism and neo-colonialism. Both parties were of the opinion that there could be no lasting world peace unless a resolute struggle was waged against the imperialist policies of aggression and war. Accordingly both parties pledged their full support for the anti-imperialist and anti-colonialist struggle in Africa, Asia and Latin America. Both parties agreed that all anti-colonialist movements in the world should close their ranks and wage a united struggle against the forces of imperialism, colonialism and neo-colonialism. It was considered that the convening of an Afro-Asian/Latin American/People's Anti-imperialism Conference was desirable, and that the possibilities for such a conference should be explored. It was also considered that an Afro-Asian Conference was necessary and that active preparations should be made to convene it. Both parties were greatly encouraged by the significant progress which had already been achieved in the anti-colonialist struggle. In Africa a large number of countries had

7

already gained their independence and there were bright prospects of still others coming to swell the number. There were, nevertheless, a number of areas on the African continent where the forces of colonialism showed very little sign of yielding. Both parties expressed firm support for the peoples of Angola, Basutoland, Bechuanaland, French Somaliland, Gambia, Mozambique, Northern Rhodesia, Nyasaland, Portuguese Guinea, Southern Rhodesia, South West Africa and Swaziland, who are valiantly fighting or independence and freedom. Both parties were convinced of final victory for these peoples in their struggles.

The two parties condemned the colonial rule of the South African authorities and their policy of racial discrimination and, in common with progressive mankind, supported the struggle of the South African peoples for equal rights and national liberation. Both parties called on all countries to terminate any existing relations, particularly economic relations, with the gruesome regime of South Africa.

The two parties reviewed the situation in the Congo and agreed that everything should be done for the U.N. forces to be withdrawn from the Congo. After the withdrawal of the U.N. forces from the Congo the African countries needed to heighten their vigilance against neo-colonialist intrigues in that country.

Premier Chou En-Lai solemnly indicated that in handling its relations with the African countries, China has consistently and unswervingly taken the following stand in accordance with the Five Principles of Peaceful Co-existence and the Ten Principles of the Bandung Conference: 1.It supports the African peoples in their struggle to fight imperialism and old and new colonialism and to win and safeguard national independence. 2. It supports the governments of African countries in pursuing a policy of peace, neutrality and non-alignment. 3. It supports the African peoples in their desire to bring about solidarity and unity in the manner of their own choice. 4. It supports the African countries in their efforts to settle their disputes through peaceful consultation. 5. It holds that the sovereignty of African countries should be respected by all other countries and that encroachment and interference from any quarters should be opposed.

The two parties also discussed at length the efforts of the African peoples to establish African unity. These efforts had recently culminated in the establishment of the Organisation of African Unity at the Summit Conference of African States in Addis Ababa. The Chinese side expressed its support for the efforts of the African countries and peoples to promote African unity and solidarity aimed at defending their sovereignty, territorial integrity and independence. This was essential in eradicating all forms of colonialism from Africa; ensuring the economic and cultural development of the African peoples and achieving for them a better life. The Chinese party appreciated the Ghanaian leader's active efforts to achieve liberation and unity in Africa. The Ghanaian party expressed its appreciation of the sincere sympathy which the People's Republic of China had always maintained for the African people in their struggle towards liberation and unity.

On disarmament, the two parties considered that genuine general disarmament and the complete prohibition and thorough destruction of nuclear weapons was the goal for which all peace-loving nations and peoples of the world should strive. They were ready to make unremitting effort to this end in concert with all other peace-loving nations and peoples. The Chinese side reaffirmed its support for the resolution of the Summit Conference of African States on general disarmament and the establishment of a nuclear-free zone in Africa. The two parties considered that a World Conference of Heads of Governments would be beneficial if it could be convened for the purpose of signing an international convention prohibiting the development and use of all nuclear weapons and the complete destruction of existing nuclear weapons and their stockpiles.

The two parties discussed at length the state of the Sino-Indian border dispute since the Colombo Conference of Six Non-aligned States. They noted that the Sino-Indian border situation had relaxed, and they expressed full confidence and hope over the possibility of a peaceful settlement of the Sino-Indian boundary question. The Chinese side appreciated the peaceful efforts made by Ghana and other Colombo powers. Two two parties expressed their determination to continue to support such peaceful efforts aimed at bringing about direct Sino-Indian negotiations.

Both parties declared that the foundation of good relations among all nations should be the observance of basic principles of international life, namely, mutual respect for territorial integrity and sovereignty, non-aggression, non-interference in the internal affairs of other countries, equality and mutual benefit and the solution of all international issues by negotiation. Both parties also agreed that Afro-Asian countries should settle all their disputes in accordance with the Five Principles of Peaceful Co-existence and the Ten Principles of the Bandung Conference.

The Ghanaian side re-affirmed its support for the restoration of China's legitimate rights and position in the United Nations as an indispensable requisite for the proper functioning of that Organisation, and objected to any attempts being made to create "Two Chinas."

The Chinese party, on their side, reiterated their support for increased Afro-Asian representation on United Nations bodies and agencies to reflect the growing influence of the Afro-Asian countries in international affairs, and re-affirmed that this question of increased Afro-Asian representation should not be linked in any way with the question of the restoration of Chinese rights in the United Nations.

The two leaders noted with satisfaction that significant achievements had been made in the promotion of mutual friendly relations between their two countries. Contributory to this achievement was the satisfactory implementation of the various agreements Treaty of Friendship, Agreement on Economic and Technical Co-operation, Trade and Payments Agreement and Agreement on Cultural Co-operation which were signed between the two countries during the Ghanaian leader's visit to China in 1961.

Both parties pledged their determination to strengthen further the existing bonds of friendship and mutual understanding as their joint contribution to the establishment of even greater trust among states and to the evolution of international peaceful co-operation.

Both parties were convinced that the visit of Premier Chou En-Lai to Ghana had conduced to the strengthening of the friendship between the Chinese and Ghanaian peoples and to the development of friendly and co-operative relations between the two countries, as well as to the promotion of Asian-African solidarity and the defence of world peace.

Accra.

16th January, 1964

11

A NEW ERA

BROADCAST TO THE NATION

February 3, 1964

MEN AND WOMEN OF GHANA,

The Referendum is now over, and I want to speak to you tonight and to thank you—the Chiefs and people of Ghana—for the overwhelming demonstration of your solidarity and determination, and for your faith in the goals we have set before us. Let me commend especially all the Party activists, functionaries, supporters and sympathizers who threw themselves so wholeheartedly into the campaign, as well as the officials and election staff whose honesty and sincerity made the voting so smooth and orderly.

I want to tell you what a source of encouragement and invigoration your support has been to me.

During the past week, you the people of Ghana—have given the greatest manifestation of your steadfastness and faith in the Convention People's Party—the party that led you to freedom; the party that stands for your interest, because its very existence springs from you the people. By giving your mandate once again to the party, you have demonstrated in the most positive terms our country's determination to establish a socialist society in which everyone of us will stand free and with equal opportunities in all respects with his neighbour.

Very soon, a Bill will be presented to Parliament in order to amend the Constitution on the lines which have been approved by you in this Referendum.

I have never hidden from you the fact that our struggle is a hard and complex one. It is a struggle that involves fighting on many fronts, because that struggle is not only political and economic, but social, cultural and spiritual as well. I have told you on many occasions that our struggle falls into several stages. Our first stage

12

ended when we took over the control of our own affairs as independent Ghana.

At that point, our party resolved to pass on to the next stage of our struggle–the construction of a socialist society. We felt then that we should mobilise and employ the energies of all sections of the community, because we took it for granted that everyone, in all walks of life, would consider it a privilege and duty to unite on a national basis in such a noble cause.

In the reconstruction of our country, however, we have found that certain elements in our society maliciously refuse to see eye to eye with us, even though in their heart of hearts they know that the course we have taken is the right one.

By joining forces with the neo-colonialists, these elements infiltrated into the organs which administer and direct our State, and tried to corrupt our Judiciary and our Police. To some extent they succeeded, and it was the measure of your vigilance that the country rallied quickly from the shock of Kulungugu and the subsequent acts of terrorism which were planned to break your confidence in the national cause, and to bring discord and disharmony into the country.

The latest sequence of events, from the treason trial to the assassination attempt at Flagstaff House on the 2nd of January this year, has made it imperative that we should uproot completely all the forces of intrigue, subversion and violence designed to deflect us from our chosen goal.

It means that we must dig out the traitors and saboteurs and bring them to answer for their misdeeds. We must take the firmest measures against those who are bent on undermining our economic and social stability. Bribery, corruption and other social vices are evils that injure our stability and impede our progress. We must therefore make serious efforts to wipe out these evils from our society. At this new stage of our national life, let us put an end to the string of malicious lying and rumour-mongering fomented by evil men and neo-colonialist agents amongst us. By their own deeds they shall be smoked out one by one.

13

Above all, we must entrust the organs of the State to those upon whom we can rely to carry out our purposes and policies in accordance with our aims and aspirations. We shall see to it that the Civil Service, our Public Boards and Corporations and State Enterprises, and all other agencies of our Government, are operated by honest and dedicated men and women.

The state is now set for us to embark upon the next phase in our struggle, to bring about a better way of living. This is the revolutionary stage in which the needs and aspirations of the people shall be supreme. This stage demands that everyone within our society must either accept the spirit and aims of our revolution, or expose themselves as the deceivers and betrayers of the people. The way is now clear for us to go forward to create the conditions in which every one of us shall enjoy the benefits of adequate food and protection, education, medical attention, proper housing, and all the other amenities which make life work living.

It was in order to mark this revolutionary stage in our struggle, that we sought to amend our Constitution and bring it in line with the social purpose and social structure upon which it should be based. You have given your consent—over-whelmingly. I congratulate you on this massive manifestation of your understanding of our high purpose; and I have confidence in your ability to see that this is carried through.

As from to-day, Ghana has entered upon a new era. You have put the Party in a new strategic position in relation to yourselves. By your unequivocal "Yes" vote, you have, in the most emphatic way, expressed your belief not simply in the Convention People's Party, but in yourselves and in the nation.

It is because we have faith in ourselves to overcome our enemies at home and abroad, that we have agreed to rest the power of the State in the hands of the people. It is because we recognise that we, the people, can best serve as the watchmen of our interests, that we have voted ourselves as the guardians of the State. For that is what we are really saying when we say that "the people are the source of power and the guardians of the State." From whom else could power possibly spring but from the people?

The Party is the rallying point of our political activity. Without the Party there would be no force through which to focus the needs and the desires of the people. The Convention People's Party is this force. The Party, therefore, is the hard core of those who are so dedicated to its ideology and programme, that they take their membership as the most serious business of their lives. The Party is nothing but the political vanguard of the people, the active organ of the people, working at all times in the service of the people.

All of us are now one in the acceptance of a One-Party State. Our task is to plan for progress in the interests of the whole people. To carry out this work of service to the people, the Party needs the assistance of everybody, even those who are not members. The assistance the Party asks of all of us—men and women of Ghana—is that we should give of our very best in whatever work we do. If we do this, we will be helping the Party and thereby satisfying the people's needs and hopes. As long as we carry out these obligations, we can rest assured that we are doing the right thing and that no one can interfere with us. For we shall be interpreting the constitutional rights and duties vested in us as the source of power and the guardians of the State.

Our Parliament has now become a corporate body made up of Party members voted in by the people as their representatives. Thus Parliament is the corporate representative of the people. As such, it will exercise the rights of the people as a unified body, working for the prosperity of Ghana and the happiness and welfare of the individuals who make up our nation. Like the Party itself, we expect Parliament to be composed of farmers and workers, artisans, factory workers, teachers, technicians, engineers, managers, intellectuals and university professors, doctors, members of the civil service, of public boards and corporations and of the judiciary—in short, people from every sector of our public life. Parliamentary service should not be a career, a means of furthering the ambitions of either individuals or special interests.

To represent the people in Parliament is a privilege, a privilege of which we must be worthy. The privilege of representing the people in Parliament and in Government does not endow Parliamentarians with special attributes that should set them above the people. On the contrary, in putting ourselves forward to represent the people in Parliament, we accept the most responsible of duties, that of expressing and carrying out the will of people in the highest forum of their representation. To do this we need to remain close to the people. The greatest sin we can commit is to lose touch with the people or place ourselves in behaviour above them. The people's Parliamentarians are the executors of the people's will, and will be trusted to perform their function only as long as they are doing so sincerely, honestly and devotedly.

These are some of the important ways by which we shall ensure that the well-being of the people remains the primary consideration in our plans and their implementation. Steps have already been taken to rid the protective arms of our State of the people's enemies. We shall take other serious and energetic steps to deal with the many evils and vices which are hampering our progress and have tended to open conflicts in our society.

From to-day we, the people, must resolve to keep our ranks firmly closed against our enemies, both external and internal, and to assign ourselves the solemn duty of protecting our State. The violence that these enemies have hurled against us has failed utterly. It has in reality recoiled upon the perpetrators themselves. We have now been brought even closer together; our determination has been rekindled and we take up the challenge of forging ahead against all odds towards the goal before us.

Vigilance must be our watchword. We must keep a keen eye on all anti-social activities. We are determined that racketeers shall not profit from the people's needs. All-out efforts are being made to see that essential commodities are available in adequate quantities to meet the ordinary needs of the people.

The mainspring of our society in the past has been its community sense, the obligation of one to another. It is around this mainspring that our African society was organised, and it is this mainspring that must continue to motivate our society in the present. For the identification of the well-being of one with the well-being of all is the animating principle of socialism. The difference is that socialism in the modern world can only establish itself on the basis of plenty. And it is towards the achievement of plenty that the Party has geared itself. It is for the achievement of plenty and its fair distribution among the people that our Seven-Year Plan is designed.

What the party has done for the masses since you, the people, voted it into power, is only the beginning of the greater things we can expect. But our hopes cannot be realised unless all of us work in the spirit of devotion and self-sacrifice.

By your vote you have indicated overwhelmingly your readiness to participate and to protect the gains that have already been made.

You have shown to the world the unity of purpose and determination that binds us, as Ghanaians, together. United as we are around a common purpose and a common destiny, we shall work steadfastly and harmoniously for a greater Ghana in which the welfare and happiness of each and every one of us shall be the dominating aim.

Goodnight to you all.

5

BLUE PRINT OF OUR GOAL

LAUNCHING THE
SEVEN -YEAR DEVELOPMENT PLAN

11th March, 1964

MR. SPEAKER, MEMBERS OF THE NATIONAL ASSEMBLY,

J have come here to-day to present to you, and to the people of Ghana, our Seven-Year Development Plan, which when completed, will bring Ghana to the threshold of a modern State based on a highly organised and efficient agricultural and industrial programme.

The main tasks of the Plan are: firstly, to speed up the rate of growth of our national economy. Secondly, it is to enable us to embark upon the socialist transformation of our economy through the rapid development of the State and co-operative sectors. Thirdly, it is our aim, by this Plan, to eradicate completely the colonial structure of our economy.

On this occasion, let me take the opportunity here and now to thank all those experienced men and women, Ghanaians and non-Ghanaians, who have contributed so much to the preparation of this Plan.

Mr. Speaker, when the Convention People's Party came to power in 1951, the pace of development was so slow and confused that we decided to speed it up by attempting to implement in five years the programme of reconstruction which was designed by the colonial administration to take place over a period of ten years. That programme was not a development plan. It was a collection of various individual petty projects that had to be built in preparation for future planning.

At the conclusion of this programme, it became necessary to pause for two years in order to consolidate our position. By the time we reached the stage of implementing the next phase of our programme, it had already become quite clear to us that the only real solution to the reconstruction of Ghana lay, in the long run, in the adoption of a socialist and co-operative programme for industry, and the mechanisation and diversification of our agriculture. Our hopes in this regard lay in the Volta River Project, about which I will have more to say later on.

Mr. Speaker, this Seven-Year Development Plan which I now lay before you is therefore the first really integrated and comprehensive economic plan ever drawn up for Ghana's development after a thorough examination of our needs and resources. The Plan is designed to give effect to the Party's Programme of Work and Happiness which has already been accepted by the country. It also embodies a long view of the path which should lead to a self-sustaining economy, based on socialist production and distribution. An economy balanced between industry and agriculture, providing a sufficiency of food for the people, and supporting secondary industries based on the products of our agriculture. In other words, an economy founded securely on the basis of socialist production and distribution.

Our aim, under this Plan, is to build in Ghana a socialist State which accepts full responsibility for promoting the well-being of the masses. Our national wealth must be built up and used in such a way that economic power shall not be allowed to exploit the worker in town or village, but be used for the supreme welfare and happiness of our people. The people, through the State, should have an effective share in the economy of the country and an effective control over it.

A socialist Ghana must also secure for every citizen, at the earliest possible date, an adequate level of education and nutrition and a satisfactory standard of clothing, housing and leisure.

The Party has always proclaimed socialism as the objective of our social, industrial and economic programmes. Socialism, however, will continue to remain a slogan until industrialisation is achieved. Socialism demands a very different kind of planning and economic structure from the type that was evolved by the colonial administration. This is why in 1961 we set up a Planning Commission and charged it with the responsibility for drawing up this Development Plan which I present to you to-day as an

19

instalment in the process by which we hope to turn Ghana into the sort of country we envisage.

A socialist State cannot come by itself, nor can it be established by the formulation of plans. Socialism has to be worked for and even sacrificed for. Socialism, which is aimed at the emancipation of the people from exploitation, has to be built by the people. It is the expression of the people whose Government accepts responsibility for promoting their welfare to the fullest possible extent.

Our youth from the primary schools, through the secondary schools to the universities and higher institutions of learning, should and must be taught and trained in the socialist philosophy. They must be taught to know the working of neo-colonialism and trained to recognise it wherever it may rear its head. They must not only know the trappings of colonialism and imperialism, but they must also be able to smell out the hide-outs of neo-colonialism.

In this endeavour, we shall expect from each citizen a maximum contribution to the national economy according to his ability and training. It is only in proportion to the contribution which each of us makes to the work of the Nation that we can expect to share in the material gains which the socialist development of the economy will make possible.

Mr. Speaker, in order to accomplish our objectives, we have decided that the economy of Ghana will, for some time to come, remain a mixed economy in which a vigorous public and co-operative sector will operate along with the private sector. Let me make it clear that our socialist objectives demand that the public and co-operative sector of the productive economy should expand at the maximum possible rate, especially in those strategic areas of production upon which the economy of the country essentially depends.

We are determined that the economic independence of Ghana shall be achieved and maintained so as to avoid the social antagonisms resulting from the unequal distribution of economic power. We are equally determined to ensure that the operation of a mixed economy leads to the socialist transformation we envisage, and not to the defeat of our socialist aims. It is essential, therefore, that we should remind ourselves at all times of the necessity

firstly, to promote to the maximum the development of the State and co-operative sectors;

secondly, to regulate the pattern of State investment in order to give the highest priority to productive investment, and

thirdly, to determine and direct the forms and conditions of foreign investment, in order to safeguard our socialist policy and national independence.

In this way, we shall ensure that the growth rate of the public and co-operative sector of our economy will exceed the growth rate of the private sector, particularly in industry and agriculture.

Mr. Speaker, as you know, we have already established many industrial projects and enterprises, as a means of securing our economic independence and assisting in the national control of the economy. I must make it clear that these State Enterprises were not set up to lose money at the expense of the tax payers. Like all business undertakings, they are expected to maintain themselves efficiency, and to show profits. Such profits should be sufficient to build up capital for further investment as well as to finance a large proportion of the public services which it is the responsibility of the State to provide.

In every socialist country, state enterprises provide the bulk of State revenues, and we intend to follow the same pattern here. Our State Enterprises will be set yearly financial and production targets so that they may work towards definite objectives and goals and thereby given every stimulus to operate efficiently and profitably. Hence, the managers of our State Enterprises, and those in charge of our State organisations and apparatus should be men trained in management; honest and dedicated men; men with integrity; men who are incorruptible.

When we have succeeded in establishing these principles, Government will then be in a position to lower taxes progressively, to lessen steadily the burden of taxation on the people and eventually to abolish many of them, if not all of them.

I have set up a State Management Committee to bring these ideas to life and to help in building up strong, well managed, efficient and profitable State enterprises.

I intend, however, that the State Management Committee shall do more than that. I want to ensure that the people of this country are fully informed of Government's intentions and plans, particularly with regard to industrialisation and agriculture. The people have every right to be fully informed in order that they may know what our objectives are, what progress we are making and how Government funds are being spent in the interest of this country's economic development.

I am convinced that with this knowledge will come that understanding which will give our people the necessary impetus to do all they can to help achieve our objectives for work and happiness and accelerated development.

Mr. Speaker, foreign investment as the private sector of our industrial development can play an important role in our economy. It has a valuable contribution to make to our economy and to the attainment of certain specific objectives. Among these will be production of consumer goods, the local processing of Ghanaian raw material and the utilization of Ghana's natural resources in those lines of economic activity were a large volume of investment is required.

We expect, however, that such investments will not be operated so as to exploit our people. On the contrary, we expect such enterprises to assist in the expansion of the economy of the country in line with our general objectives. Foreign investment enterprises will contribute personal initiative, managerial ability and technical skills towards the development of the country. They will also further the growth of similar initiative, ability, technical skills and habits of saving among Ghanaians.

We welcome foreign investors in a spirit of partnership. They can earn their profits here, provided they leave us an agreed portion for promoting the welfare and happiness of our people as a whole as against the greedy ambitions of the few. From what we get out of this partnership, we hope to be able to expand the health services of our people, to feed and house them well, to give them more and better educational institutions and to see to it that they have a rising standard of living. This in a nutshell is what we expect from our socialist objectives.

Mr. Speaker, in pursuing these objectives, we shall exert our efforts towards the maximum extension of the public sector within the productive economy. As I have said, within this framework we do not intend or desire to limit private investme ·'.

Our Government has always insisted that ti..: operations of all economic enterprises in Ghana should conform to the national economic objectives and be subject to the rules and regulations which are made in pursuance of our socialist policies. Our experience has been that foreign investors have been willing to invest in Ghana so long as the limits within which they can work are fair and clearly defined, and we shall continue to consult with them in order to ensure that co-operation is as full as possible.

Ghana's economy, particularly at the present stage, has room for all the investment capital which is likely to be provided by foreign investors, by the Central and Local Governments and by individual Ghanaians. In this respect, I believe that there are a considerable number of individual Ghanaians who are in a position materially to assist in finding the necessary capital for the Seven-Year Development Plan.

One of the worst features of colonialism was that it produced an unbalanced economy in which there was little room for investment of the profits which were made by expatriate firms. In colonial days it was natural that profits made in Ghana should be invested abroad. To-day the situation is entirely different. An investor who lays out his money wisely in Ghana is likely to make a larger profit than if he invested it in a more developed country. Nevertheless, old habits of investment persist and there are a considerable number of Ghanaians who still maintain their savings in foreign investments and in property outside Ghana.

Under our Exchange Control laws it is, of course, illegal for Ghanaians to have property abroad without having declared this to the appropriate authorities. This aspect of our law is not always

23

understood. The Government has therefore decided, not to penalise any Ghanaian firm or individual who, within the next three months, repatriates foreign holdings of money to Ghana, or who declares ownership of foreign property. A thorough investigation is afoot to discover the extent of holdings of foreign exchange and properties by Ghanaians, and those who do not take advantage of this offer but continues to conceal their foreign assets, must expect, after the three-month period of grace, to be subject to the full rigours of the law.

Mr. Speaker, The Seven-Year Development Plan makes provisions for a maximum volume of investment from all sources.

We intend that the State should retain control of the strategic branches of the economy, including public utilities, raw materials and heavy industry. The State will also participate in light and consumer goods industries in which the rates of return on capital should be highest. We intend also that those industries which provide the basic living needs of the people shall be State-owned, in order to prevent any exploitation.

Mr. Speaker, Members of the National Assembly, let me now turn to the specific proposals of the Seven-Year Plan.

In the next seven years, it is proposed that there will be a total expenditure of one-thousand-and sixteen million pounds, that is, over a billion pounds sterling, on development projects in the Plan. Of this total, it is intended that four-hundred-and·seventy-six million pounds should be provided by the Central Government. Foreign investors, individual Ghanaians, Local Authorities and the Co-operative sector are expected to invest about four-hundred-and-forty million pounds. We also hope that individual Ghanaians will contribute nearly one-hundred million pounds worth of direct labour in the construction of buildings, in community development and in the extension of their farms.

The total government investment will be four-hundred-and-seventy-six million pounds.

Investment throughout the Seven-Year Plan period will average one-hundred-and-thirty million pounds a year. Of this, approximately

24

one half, or sixty-six million pounds a year, will be invested by Government, and the rest by private investors.

We continue to look to the outside world to contribute to our national development. We expect the more advanced and industrialised countries to facilitate our trade in primary commodities and manufactured goods so that we can finance the bulk of our development out of our own resources and earnings.

We hope that where necessary, the Government of Ghana will be able to borrow money on reasonable terms for essential and productive projects. Let me say again that we welcome foreign investors to come and invest in Ghana's progress. We offer them every assistance, substantial material benefits, and the advantages of a coherent long-term economic strategy which will give them plenty of scope for planning and development. At the same time we expect them to re-invest an adequate share of their profits in the further progress, both of Ghana and of themselves.

In order to be able to manage these new investments as well as our existing capital with the maximum of efficiency, the country needs a well-trained labour force under competent management. In this sense, the educational programme under the Plan is crucial to the success of the whole Plan. It is directed towards giving education in Ghana a new and more practical orientation and making it available to all who can profit by it. In order to make real economic progress, Ghana must adopt an improved technology in all lines of production. We look to the educational system and educational institutions to equip our people with the latest advancements in industrial and agricultural technology. We expect our Academy of Sciences and our research organisations to adapt this technology to the conditions of Ghana. And we look to the Managers of our enterprises to adopt the technology which is developed, and to foster skills by a maximum programme of "on the job" training.

The development of Ghana has hitherto not been sufficiently balanced between different parts of the country. It is the deliberate policy of this Plan to correct this imbalance. Naturally we must develop in each part of the country the type of economic activity to which it is best suited by reason of natural resources and geographical location. But a special effort has to be made in order to ensure that the rate of progress in the less favoured parts of the country is even greater than the rate of progress in those sections which have hitherto been more favoured. It is only by this means that we can achieve a more harmonious national development.

In the present Plan period it is proposed to pay special attention to the modernising of agriculture in the savannah areas of the Northern and Upper Regions. It is hoped through secondary industries based on agricultural raw material, to turn the Northern areas into major sources of food supplies for the whole country. In this regard, the Government has recognised the importance of irrigation and water conservation in the country, and has already initiated far-reaching plans for major schemes of irrigation and water conservation. Mr. Speaker, the backbone of Ghana's agriculture has always been its farmers who, particularly in recent years, have made a fine contribution to the economy and expressed their patriotism in a number of unselfish ways. The developments the Government is proposing in the areas of State and co-operative farming will bring them a share of the local facilities they have so long been denied. More than this: they will have the opportunity also to share in the up-to-date techniques of farming that must be employed if greater yields and diversity of crops are to be attained.

I want our farmers to understand that the State Farms and Co-operative enterprises are not being encouraged as alternatives to peasant farming. The interests of individual peasant farmers will not be made subservient to those of the State Farms and Co-operatives. We need the efforts of our individual farmers more than ever, along with our State Farms and Co-operatives, if we are to achieve, at an increased pace, the agricultural targets we have set ourselves. We look to our individual peasant farmers for the enlargement of investment in our agriculture.

Mr. Speaker, as I have stressed time and again, the revolution taking place in Ghana is chiefly a revolution of the workers and the tillers of the land. A vital phase of this revolution is the implementation of the Seven-Year Development Plan which aims at the total expansion of all sections of our economy to raise the standard of living of the people of Ghana. I am happy that the workers have demonstrated their complete dedication to our revolutionary cause.

Upon the attainment of independence, the Party, as the conscious political vanguard of the Trade Union Movement, worked with the Trade Unions and created a new and more effective structure of the Trades Union Congress. Government supported the desire of the workers for this new Trade Union structure.

Thus, we were able to create in our labour and industrial laws conditions for resolving quickly and expeditiously the problems of our working population. This, also, the workers accepted the responsibility to contribute to the economic and social reconstruction of our economy.

In the State sector of our economy, the workers employed in our State Corporations will be afforded full and equal opportunities for participating in the planning and execution of our industrial projects. It is only in this way that the workers will closely identify themselves with the attainment of the economic and social objectives of our new society and will thus equate their own welfare with the prosperity of our country. Such new working relationships will enable the workers to acquire the sense of complete belonging and full participation and they will no longer consider themselves as working for colonialist exploiters. I have given instructions that some of our State enterprises be handed over completely to the workers who will manage them for themselves on behalf of the State.

The success of this Seven-Year Development Plan will only be attained if the enthusiasm of our workers is mobilized and they know the part they ought to play and are drawn into full consultation in the execution of our Plan.

I therefore call upon all workers, farmers, fishermen and peasants of our country to accept this challenge and fulfil the hopes and aspirations of our people.

Mr. Speaker, when I spoke at the opening of the Unilever Soap Factory at Tema on the 24th August, 1963, I said, among other things, that in order to pay tribute to the importance of labour in the development of Ghana, the Government has decided to institute a special Order to be known as the "Order of the Black Star of Labour." Details of this Order, which will rank among the highest honours of the State, have now been worked out and all classes of labour will qualify for this Order. It is my confident expectation that this award will provide an ample incentive to all workers, and that every worker of the nation will make it his ambition to qualify for the title of Worker of the Year and to become heroes and heroines of Labour.

Mr. Speaker, Members of the National Assembly, I am happy to inform the House that on present estimates, it is confidently expected that the Volta River Project will begin to generate electrical power by September, 1965. On that date, we shall come to the end of one phase of our cherished goal and usher in the beginning of a new and more exciting endeavour to utilise the vast electric power which will be at the country's disposal for the enrichment of our economy and our people.

Completion of the Volta Project will enable us to develop the industrial potential of Ghana. Indeed, the possibilities for our agriculture and industry will be completely revolutionised. First and foremost the Volta Project will increase by nearly 500 per cent the installed electrical capacity of the country. Nearly one half of this new capacity will be taken up by the aluminium smelter in Tema. But there will be an ample reserve of power for other users, and Ghana will have liberated herself decisively from the possibility of power shortage becoming again a brake on the rate of economic progress.

I would like in this context to point out the degree to which the Volta Scheme fits into our chosen combination of a mixed economy with socialist and co-operative goals. A major part of the scheme is being financed by the Ghana Government; but the American and British Governments have joined in the financing of it, together with the World Bank, and we have had the most helpful and fruitful collaboration with American enterprise in the shape of the Kaiser Group of Industries.

Meanwhile, our Italian contractors, Impregilo, have achieved the remarkable feat of taking one year off the time of construction of the dam. Throughout the scheme, we have worked together in the greatest harmony. I regard this great scheme as an example of the way in which careful and proper planning together with foreign investment, public control and participation, and the devoted labours

28

of the people can revolutionize the economic base of society.

Such an achievement can have a significance far beyond Ghana's frontiers. It is only by strengthening our economy in this way that we can make an effective contribution to our brothers in Africa and the political unification of our continent. In this endeavour, the Seven-Year Plan makes provision for the undertaking of joint enterprises in individual fields of industry and also for the harmonisation of our total programme of economic development with that of other African countries.

The Plan we are launching to-day relates to projects and developments which we wish to see take place in Ghana. It grieves me that we in Ghana, who so strongly advocates the unity of the African Continent, should be forced to take so narrow a view of planning. I have advocated for closer union of Africa times without number. I have emphasised the need for a continental union Government for Africa as the only solution to Africa's ills and problems. Since the Addis Ababa Conference, it has been made abundantly clear that artificial borders which we inherited from the colonial powers should be made obsolete and unnecessary. While we wait for the setting up of a Union Government for Africa, we must begin immediately to harmonize our plans for Africa's total development. For example, I see no reason why the independent African States should not, with advantage to each other, join together in an economic union and draw up together a joint Development Plan which will give us greater scope and flexibility to our mutual advantage. By the same token, I see no reason why the independent African States should not have common shipping and air lines in the interest of improved services and economy. With such rationalisation of our economic policies, we could have common objectives and thus eliminate unnecessary competition and frontier barriers and disputes.

As every day passes, it is becoming clearer and clearer that it is only the establishment of a Union Government of Africa which can save our separate States not only from neo-colonialism, but from imperialism itself. We in Ghana are determined to make our whole-hearted contribution towards this objective. We are prepared to make whatever further provisions may be required to enable us to play our part in the achievement and consolidation of African Unity.

Recent events in East Africa and in other parts of Africa have shown how urgent is the need for the establishment of a central machinery for dealing with the serious political and economic questions confronting us in Africa to-day.

Mr. Speaker, Members of the National Assembly, the object of the Seven-Year Plan which I have out-lined to you is to modernise our agriculture and develop our industry as a basis of our socialist society. I, for my part, am determined that the Plan shall succeed. Its success must rest on the support of each and every one of you and on the devotion and hard work of the officials, Heads of Corporations and Enterprises, whose duty it will be to translate the Plan into action. In the seven years ahead, all our energies must be concentrated on its implementation.

It has long been apparent that the administrative machinery which we inherited was not designed for a country working within the framework of an overall plan, and in which the activities of individual agencies of the nation are directed to clearly defined goals of development. An effective reform of the governmental machinery is therefore needed if the Seven-Year Plan is not to falter on the inadequacies of administration. The first task in this regard will be to attune more closely the policies and actions of every agency or organ of Government to the overall national policy as defined in the Seven-Year Development Plan.

I have caused to be published with the Seven-Year Plan a guide to its implementation. This guide should be studied most carefully by Members of this House, by the Party and Government officials, Managers of State Enterprises, the farmers' organisation, the Trades Union Congress and all those who will be concerned with the implementation of the Plan.

I have, earlier this month, established several organisations whose responsibility it will be to see to the rapid execution of the Plan. These are, firstly, the *National Planning Commission*, through which the people will be associated with the Plan, and which will be enlarged to include Ministers, Regional Commissioners, representatives of Corporations and organisations and integral wings of the Party.

Secondly, the *State Planning Committee* which, under my Chairmanship, will be the key body for co-ordinating action and policy on the Plan, and for giving directions on its execution and implementation.

Thirdly, there is the *Budget Committee*, which will make recommendations for the policy of the annual budget.

Fourthly, the *Foreign Exchange Committee*, which will make recommendations regarding the size of yearly imports and exports.

And lastly though by no means the least there is the *State Management Committee* which will direct the operations and activities of State Corporations and State Enterprises in order to ensure their efficient and profitable management.

I am sure that if these five bodies carry out their duties honestly and energetically, we shall achieve and even exceed our goals under this Plan. We might even complete the Plan ahead of schedule, that is to say in less than seven years.

Mr. Speaker, all our efforts should henceforth be directed to ensuring that everything is done to make this Plan a success. I am sure that all the people of this country are determined in their efforts to ensure that we achieve all our Plan objectives and make our country a happy, progressive, prosperous and advanced nation. We must therefore ensure that State funds and resources are not frittered away uselessly or wastefully or that they find their way into private pockets.

We shall, in order to implement the Plan, be awarding a number of contracts to organisations both here and abroad; we shall also be entering into sales agreements as well as acquiring goods locally. I intend that all contracts, whether for the construction of factories or offices, or for any purchase or sale, should be so safeguarded that our funds will be properly husbanded and utilised for Ghana's advancement and for the welfare and happiness of the people.

In order that our resources are not waste by corrupt practices and in order to prevent any attempts at personal greed and aggrandisement at the expense of the people and the State, steps will be taken to ensure that no contractor . hall offer or give or agree to give to any person in the service of the Government of Ghana any gift or consideration of any kind as an inducement or reward for doing, or forbearing to do, or for having done any act in relation to the obtaining or execution of any contract for the Government of Ghana, or for showing favour or disfavour to any person in relation to any other contract for the Government of Ghana.

We shall also see to it that no contractor shall enter into any contract with the Government of Ghana in connection with which a commission has been paid or agreed to be paid by him or on his behalf, or to his knowledge, unless before the contract is made, particulars of any such commission and of the terms and conditions of any agreement for the payment thereof have been disclosed in writing to a special committee to be appointed by me to represent the Government of Ghana.

Any breach of these conditions shall entitle the Government to determine any contract, and recover from the contractor the amount of any loss which may have resulted from such determination and the amount or value of any such gifts, consideration or commission.

I have therefore directed that every contract for the supply of goods and services or for the execution of any Government project shall embody clauses to give effect to this decision. These conditions are being made in the interest of the tax payer who ultimately has to find the money to pay for these gifts and bribes.

I want the world to know that we shall do everything to set our own house in order. I want all of us here in Ghana also to realise that nothing must be allowed to hamper our efforts to achieve our Plan objectives and that no individuals will be permitted to hamper that effort, to retard our advancement in any way or to grow rich by corrupt practices. Those who have ears to hear, let them hear. The progress, welfare and happiness of the masses is our supreme concern.

Mr. Speaker, we know that the desire of people is to have enough to eat without spending too great a part of their income upon food. They want a reasonably comfortable place to sleep; they want light, a ready supply of water, education for the growing children and future generation, adequate medical care and welfare services. Our present plan will go a long way to fulfiling these very legitimate desires of the people. The Volta project will provide us with abundant light and water. In addition, a whole programme of irrigation and water development is engaging our attention very seriously.

Housing, too, is one of our main preoccupations. We are at this moment in the last stages of formulating large-scale housing projects, which we hope to have ready soon. A factory for prefabricated concrete units is now under construction and will come into production sometime this year. When these plans are completed, we shall be able to put up low-cost housing to meet the needs of our working people at the rate of about two hundred houses a month. This should go a long way to offset the pressing housing problem.

In transforming the many centres of over-crowded and insanitary housing that at present exist in some areas, we shall look carefully into the traditional community customs of our people and will, wherever it is feasible and possible, try to maintain such communities in their traditional locations, but with a newer, better and more pleasant look.

Mr. Speaker, we would be hampering our advance to socialism if we were to encourage the growth of Ghanaian private capitalism in our midst. This would, of course, be in antipathy to our economic and social objectives. There are some few among us who are seeking outlets for small enterprises. Such people we appreciate have initiative which it would be well to employ suitably in our socialist undertakings. There are some who have small capital savings which they consider they can profitably employ in business that will provide goods and services which are in public demand. Such small businessmen will be encouraged to operate enterprises provided they accept certain limitations as the Government will find it necessary to impose as to the size of the enterprise and the number of persons to be employed in their undertakings.

In this connection it is necessary to distinguish between two types of business which have grown up within recent years. The first is the type which it is the Government's intention to encourage.

33

that of the small businessman who employs his capital in an industry or trade with which he is familiar, and in so doing, fulfils a public need.

The second type is very different. It consists of that class of Ghanaian businesses which are modelled on the old type of colonial exploitation. Individuals who can command capital use their money not in productive endeavour, but by the purchase and re-sale, at high prices, of such commodities as fish, salt and other items of food and consumer goods which are in demand by the people. This type of business serves no social purpose and steps will be taken to see that our banking resources are not used to provide credit for this type of business.

Even more harmful to the economy is yet another type of enterprise in which some Ghanaians have been participating. This consists of setting up bogus agencies for foreign companies which are in fact nothing but organisations for distributing bribes and exerting improper pressures on behalf of foreign companies. It is the intention of the Government to carry out a wholesale investigation into the activities of these firms. They can do incalculable harm to our economy and they must be ruthlessly suppressed.

The initiative of Ghanaian businessmen will not be cramped, but we must take steps to see that it is channelled towards desirable social ends and is not expended in the exploitation of the community. The Government will encourage Ghanaian businessmen to join with each other in co-operative forms of organisation. In this way Ghanaian businessmen will be able to contribute actively in broadening the vitality of our economy and co-operation, and will provide a stronger form of organisation than can be achieved through individual small businesses.

We must also discourage anything that can threaten our socialist construction. For this reason, no Ghanaian will be allowed to take up shares in any enterprise under foreign investment. On the contrary, we shall encourage our people with savings to invest in the State sector and co-operative undertakings. I know that among our Ghanaian businessmen, there are some who are ready and willing to turn their businesses into co-operative undertakings. Where well-run private enterprises are offered to and taken over by the State or co-operative undertakings, we hope that businessmen will offer themselves as managers and administrators.

In the same way, Mr. Speaker, I want to refer to money-lending which, along with other problems, has been left to us by colonialism. I know that many of those who are carrying on this business of lending money at criminal rates of interest are non-Ghanaians. But, unhappily, not a few of our own people have joined the ranks of those who make quick and easy money out of the difficulties and misery of others. Money-lending and usury are intolerable and inconsistent with the ideals of a socialist state. We should see to it that this practice is eliminated from our society.

Mr. Speaker, Members of the National Assembly, I am sure that imbued with the spirit of the Party's programme of Work and Happiness, all those who are responsible for the interpretation and implementation of this Plan will do their work honestly and devotedly. It may be that in the course of the next seven years some of us will from time to time attempt to change the choice of emphasis that we have made and try to direct proportionately more of our national resources into immediate welfare services and proportionately less into agriculture and industry. It will be the duty of those who are charged with the implementation of the Plan to ensure that these pressures are resisted. Otherwise we shall end up in the long run with an economy weak in its productive base and backward in its level of technology.

The Seven-Year Development Plan can only be accounted a success if by 1970 the year in which we conclude the Plan and the year in which we celebrate the Tenth Anniversary of our Republic we can truly say that the productive base of the economy has been revolutionised and that the level of technology and productivity in Ghana is approaching modern standards over the adequate area of the national economy.

Mr. Speaker, Members of the National Assembly, 1964, the year in which we launch the Seven-Year Development Plan, will be hailed as the turning point in the history of Ghana. In a little over a year from now, we shall be generating electricity from the Volta River Project to feed our expanding factories throughout the country. The Kwame Nkrumah Steel Works in Tema will soon be completed. Tema Harbour itself is already being extended to meet the needs of our expanding economy, and in Tema a growing number of industrial projects are already in production and more are being established. In this connection I want to mention, particularly, the Aluminium Smelter which will produce aluminium for domestic consumption and export, the Dry Dock and Ship Repair Yard which will be one of the finest and biggest in Africa and the Accra Tema Freeway, which will provide fast and safe travelling between the capital and the port of Tema.

I can already see, in my mind's eye, a picture of Ghana as it will be by the end of the Plan period. I see a State with a strong and virile economy, its agriculture and industry bouyant and prosperous, an industrialised nation serving the needs of its people.

Let us therefore, as from to-day, move forward together, united in devotion and determination, to give of our best in the execution and implementation of this Seven-Year Plan.

Mr. Speaker, Members of the National Assembly, it gives me a great pleasure on this historic occasion, and in this House, to launch our Seven-Year Development Plan.

I now leave you to your deliberations. May you continue to be guided by Providence in the highest interests of our Nation.

6

SYMBOL OF GOODWILL AND FRIENDSHIP

DINNER IN HONOUR OF OSAGYEFO BY THE DIPLOMATIC CORPS

May 23, 1964

MR. DEAN,
MEMBERS OF THE DIPLOMATIC CORPS,
LADIES AND GENTLEMEN,

J wish to thank you, the members of the Diplomatic Corps, for your kind gesture in arranging this Dinner in my honour. I recall that memorable and happy occasion last year when I was your guest at a similar function. The sharing of a common meal as we have done tonight, is a symbol of goodwill and friendship, and I am happy to think that such goodwill and friendship can strengthen and promote the relations between Ghana and the countries which you represent here.

You, Mr. Dean, have just referred to the large diplomatic representation in Ghana to-day. More than half the nations of the world have decided to establish diplomatic relations with us. I like to feel that this is not only a tribute to Ghana, but also an indication of the interest that these nations have in the policies we pursue, as well as the way in which we manage our own affairs. I thank those of you who have an unbiassed understanding of our problems and policies and who try to interpret them accurately to their respective Governments. In doing so, you may perhaps fall short of the standards believed to have been set at one time by the conventional diplomat who was sent abroad to "lie" for the good of his country.

Ladies and Gentlemen: goodwill is perhaps the greatest need in the world today. It is the chief duty of the diplomat to do everything in his power to promote international understanding. And the first step in this direction is to get acquainted with the history, customs and way of life of the people in the country to which he has been

37

assigned. It is only when he really gets to know the country and its people that he can be in a position to distinguish fact from fiction. It is most important that he should be able to do this. And more important still, that he has the courage to come out boldly in defence of facts when he recognises that they have been distorted. For the sake of goodwill and complete understanding between the countries he is concerned with, he must ensure that news items are presented to his own people correctly and objectively.

I can recall not so long ago that you, Mr. Dean, remarked to me that the Diplomatic Corps, did not see enough of me in the course of their duties. I fear that as your numbers grow, it may become more and more difficult for us to meet individually as often as you may wish. That is why we must all welcome a Dinner like this, which gives us a good opportunity to meet one another and to share our thoughts in a friendly and happy atmosphere. Nevertheless, it is not easy, at such a gathering, to express ourselves frankly and freely on the problems facing our individual countries and the world without saying anything which might be construed as a criticism of the policies of one or other of the fifty-two countries whom you represent here in Ghana.

Anyway, I will try; it will at least provide me with an exercise in diplomacy.

You, Mr. Dean, have also emphasised in your speech that we should not excuse our shortcomings on the grounds that history repeats itself. We must admit that history only seems to repeat itself, it is the historians who repeat each other, and thus determine the attitudes of mind from which contemporary problems are viewed.

When we in Africa look at the world to-day, we are often struck by the double standards which are frequently applied in dealing with the problems of our continent.

For example, some of the former colonial powers still believe in a policy of divide and rule by which they consider that political difficulties in other parts of the world can be solved. And so, whenever there appear different political views in any one country, they always seek a solution by dividing that country into two. The only inconsistency in the application of this dead theory is that none of the nations advocating it have ever applied it to their own country. In other words, they believe in unity at home, but are Balkanizers abroad.

Let me refer to another example of double standards. For a long time, diplomatic thinking has been dominated by the idea of maintaining the balance of power. Peace, it was thought, could be preserved by ensuring that no nation became either too powerful or too weak in a world of rivalry and competing claims. Such a theory demanded, for instance, that if a great power disappeared, then the balance of power could only be maintained by dividing up its former territories into small States. These States would then be bound to come under the influence of one or other of the great powers, and thus the balance of power would be maintained. The partition of Africa was made frankly for this purpose. None of the great powers at the Berlin Conference of 1885 considered the effect of their decisions. They had no regard for any arguments based on the economic, social or ethnic groupings in Africa. They were solely concerned to see that there was a balance of power among the metropolitan powers who had carved up Africa into the strange jig-saw puzzle which it pleased them to refer to as "spheres of influence." This laboriously constructed balance of power in Africa did not, however, prevent the great powers from indulging in two major world wars.

In our effort to unite Africa to-day, we are still bearing the burden of this baneful and iniquitous decision. One would have thought that their experience in this alone would have shown the Powers the futility of the theory of the balance of power as a factor for preserving peace. But no—even after the Second World War the great nations of the world still pursued this phantasy and illusion.

In my view, far from partition and balkanisation being a stabilising factor, it is one of the greatest dangers to world peace.

In the nineteenth century the great powers outside Africa believed erroneously that they could secure their own safety and economic security by dividing up the African Continent. Little did they realise then that their economic and political interests could be enhanced if they had fostered African unity. It is therefore not too much to call upon the powers of to-day to assist in making the unity of Africa possible. Indeed, the political unification of Africa is the most urgent and decisive issue of our time.

It is to the advantage of the African States to have a large enough internal market to sustain the effective industrialisation of the Continent. If the industrialised nations of the world are to export their capital goods to Africa, they can only find a strong and stable market for such exports in a unified African economic area. Lever Brothers saw this point economically years ago and created the great economic octopus of the United Africa Company. They even have Africa House in London!

The age of the hoe and the camel is past and gone forever. Africa, in common with other countries of the world, is already in the age of the tractor and the jet plane. We therefore have to think in terms of the optimum areas of development and population. A united Africa, with a union government of its own, will provide this optimum land mass and optimum population. The countries which you represent, with their vast growing industrial complexes, particularly in Europe, America and Russia, will surely prefer to trade with a politically stable and united Africa, with its great economic and material resources, rather than with numerous weak states with fragile economic and unstable governments within a multitude of disputable frontier barriers. Africa's population—even with the inadequacies of our census systems—now stands at 300 million, with a cohesive and compact land mass covering an area of 12 million square miles.

Mr. Dean, recently the world press has made much of the bombing of "dissident tribesmen." On this occasion, I do not wish to discuss such a controversial issue as this. As you know, we in Ghana do not even give legal recognition to the existence of tribes or of tribal groups. I would only like to ask why those who have to deal with the people they call "dissident tribesmen" do not apply their methods impartially.

If one looks round the African Continent the most obvious example of a group who could be referred to as "dissident tribesmen" are the white settlers of Southern Rhodesia. They have peculiar attributes. They are a small minority, less than 6 per cent of

40

the population of Southern Rhodesia. They, like the so-called Afrikaaners of South Africa, believe in maintaining their tribal position by force. They obstinately maintain social and religious barriers between themselves and the rest of the population. They even refuse to inter-marry with the people among whom they are living. Suppose these settlers in Southern Rhodesia are able to overthrow the Constitution and proclaim themselves as the rulers of the country, what then? Will they be treated in the same way as other "dissident tribesmen" have been treated elsewhere? I cannot of course advocate the solution of the Southern Rhodesia problem by the bombing of the clearly defined and segregated white tribal lands of Southern Rhodesia. I am against the bombing of all tribesmen irrespective of their colour.

If the solution by bombing is to be ruled out, what then? It seems to me that in the case of both Southern Rhodesia and South Africa, a kind of paralysis of will affects many of the great nations of the world. They all acknowledge that the system of apartheid and racial discrimination practised in these countries is not only morally wrong, but is in itself a threat to world peace. Yet on these particular issues on which the world is practically unanimous, there is a singular failure to take effective action, because their economic and financial interests are involved.

Moral scruples appear to overtake many countries when asked to take action on African matter, although these same scruples do not seem to trouble them when dealing with their own affairs. For example, why cannot the decisions of the United Nations in regard to South Africa be implemented by the establishment of a blockade? If one looks at the arguments against this course they would seem to be based not on a defence of the South African position but on the moral ground that a blockade for political reasons is improper and immoral. Yet, if one looks round the world, one sees attempts to organise commercial blockades to enforce a change of regime upon countries whose political systems are condemned by some of their neighbours.

Surely, as members of the United Nations, we can express the international spirit fully in action by trade and other relations with member-states without sacrificing our political beliefs and our policy of non-alignment.

41

It is this double standard in approaching world problems which I believe should be condemned. The countries of the world must accept and maintain in their dealings with each other, the standards of justice and fair play. If we did this, I am sure it would not be long before problems such as we have in Laos, South Vietnam, Cyprus and in the Middle East would be solved in a spirit of mutual understanding and harmony. In the same spirit, I am convinced that it will be possible to find a solution to the burning Middle East, Arab/Israel problem one way or the other.

Mr. Dean, I am told that one of the first lessons a diplomat must learn is how to yawn with his mouth shut and how to appear keenly interested in a subject that bores him stiff. As long as you appear to me to be interested in what I'm saying, I can always keep on talking!

As far as politicians are concerned, they never shut their mouths anyhow. On the rare occasions when they do so, people view them with concern and dismay. Politicians are a much maligned set. It is said that all they do is create chaos. But if there were no politicians to make life complicated every so often, you must admit that it would be a pretty boring and humdrum existence—especially for you diplomats.

This reminds me of a story I heard recently about an architect, an engineer and a politician who were admiring a newly-built city from a hill-top. The architect, puffing out his chest and looking very self-satisfied, said to the other two: "Well, you have to admit that I did a splendid job designing that magnificent city!" "Just a minute," the engineer interrupted him. "It was I who actually did the building of it." The two of them argued the point for some time, each one claiming the credit. Then the politician got bored with listening to all this bragging, and he put an end to it by saying: "In my opinion, most of the credit should go to me. After all, if I hadn't created such a fuss in the beginning about the slums in this area, it won't have been necessary to rebuild the city at all." Mr. Dean, the dynamic impact of Africa's awakening has shaken the world. It was Ghana that first stirred that slumbering African giant. Because of this, neither Ghana nor Kwame Nkrumah has been forgiven by those whose economic and political interests are incompatible with what we stand for. We have been attacked relentlessly and mercilessly by

42

the Western press, often by journalists who have assessed the position after a few hours in Ghana spent leaning at the bar of the Ambassador Hotel. You who live among us and who know the sort of people we are, can perform a great service not only to Ghana, but to all·Africa, by letting the true facts be known and by exposing the utter irresponsibility and damage of this kind of absentee reportage. I am tolerated by the Western press "as affectionately as toothache and as tenderly as a thorn."

But it is not I or Ghana who is worried about all this. We in Ghana don't care a rap what they say about us. We know where we are going, what we want and how we are going to get there. We will not be deterred by any criticism. As Omar Khaayam wrote: "The dogs bark but the caravan moves on."

Diplomats are sometimes looked upon as being legalized international spies. I don't share that view. But inasmuch as they should keep their eyes wide open and snatch every opportunity to strengthen the ties between their country and Ghana, the more so-called spying they do the better for us all. A diplomat alive to his responsibilities can make a most valuable contribution towards the creation of public opinion. To those of you who have accorded to Ghana that understanding and friendship, I say: Thank you. To those others, I say: May you adopt a more reasonable frame of mind towards us in the future.

What are you here for, anyway? Is it not to promote friendly relations between your country and Ghana? To build up such a fund of goodwill and understanding between us that peace, friendship and co-operation are assured not only between our countries, but throughout the world. Mr. Dean, Members of the Diplomatic Corps: This is your challenge.

Members of the Diplomatic Corps, let me thank you once again for this Dinner and also for the warm sentiments in your Dean's speech. And now, Ladies and Gentlemen: will you rise with me and drink a toast—a toast to the Diplomatic Corps in Ghana.

7

SPEECH BY DIPLOMATIC CORPS

SPEECH BY HIS EXCELLENCY MR. G. FLAMMA SHERMAN, AMBASSADOR OF LIBERIA AND DEAN OF THE DIPLOMATIC CORPS AT A DINNER IN HONOUR OF OSAGYEFO

OSAGYEFO THE PRESIDENT,
MADAM FATHIA NKRUMAH,
MR. CHIEF JUSTICE AND MR. SPEAKER,
HONOURABLE MINISTERS,
DISTINGUISHED LADIES AND GENTLEMEN,

My distinguished colleagues will, undoubtedly, agree with me, Mr. President, when I say we deem it a privilege and honour to have you and Madam Fathia Nkrumah with us tonight, and are grateful to all our friends and guests who have accepted and made it possible to join us on this important occasion.

Though I have just returned from a rather protracted leave in time to play—by mere reason of diplomatic tradition—this enviable role of spokesman for my learned colleagues of the most colourful and, I believe, largest diplomatic group in Africa, yet, I must confess, Mr. President, that the credit for your long-sought acceptance and for the preliminary arrangements without which this evening's occasion would have been impossible, goes to my able friend and co-Doyen, His Excellency the Chinese Ambassador, Mr. Huang Hua, and to the Chairman of the Committee on arrangements, His Excellency the French Ambassador, Mr. Phillippe Grousset and his group.

It was, as you will recall, Mr. President, on March 6, 1963—Ghana's Independence Day—when, on a similar occasion, I had the satisfaction of referring to her rapid progress and astonishing achievements under your enlightened leadership.

Since this time—little over a year ago today–there has been, on the international scene, a forward march of events, accompanied by new and noteworthy developments. Some of these have only helped to blacken the pages of history while the others have tended to inspire hope and not despair; the success of the Addis Ababa Conference, the birth and manifest usefulness of the Organization of African Unity and the partial Nuclear Test Ban, are among the new and brighter signs. These, added to the continual endeavour of the Nuclear Powers to find agreement on total disarmament; the continued interest of the Bandung, Colombo and non-aligned countries in the peaceful settlement of international disputes, with the continuous existence of the United Nations and man's international peace–have indeed helped to sustain the hope of humanity.

But this hope, as you know, Mr. President, can fade away overnight, unless men and nations learn to benefit by the lessons of history in their true perspectives. We often try to blame history by complaining that it "repeats itself" when we know very well that the underlying factors or forces which influence and direct the course of history are principally our own feelings, thinking, attitudes and doing; for, history only mirrors the resultant consequences of the doings of men and nations alike. It is obvious that if the behaviour patterns of men and nations would modify or take a new shift in the true light of lessons of the past, history is bound to take a corresponding new course. But, if for any consideration, we would continue to either completely ignore or by organised efforts pervert the proper perspectives of history in our dealings, the result is most likely to be the same.

Experience in international relations shows clearly that most of today's great successes have their roots in the past, and that lofty ideals and principles, no matter how well conceived, and universally proclaimed, are doomed to the same fate, if superseded by the same material expediencies of the past.

Thus, Mr. President, in these days of perplexing anxieties and growing awareness that the time no longer exists when any useful purpose is served by war, it is to all of you, who bear rule in our time –whom God has endowed with great faculties and gifts of insight to weigh men and things from your positions of authority and influence –that humanity and history will look to play such decisive role today as would influence the course of world events for a better tomorrow.

45

On your own national scene, Mr. President, the march of progress in Ghana has, since that Independence Day, remained unabating. We have since witnessed, with admiration, the growth of new branches of industries, like the important Oil Refinery and Soap factories in Tema; watched the continuous progress of the great Volta River Project at Akosombo; we have in addition to the continual expansion of your shipping and other existing industries, noted the increasing emphases on Higher Education, Scientific and Technological training; the putting into effect of your New Seven-Year Development Plan, with serious programming for greater productivity; speedy industrialization to build a healthy national economy for the maximum well-being and happiness of your people.

If in these efforts of the government and people of Ghana to build a great and prosperous nation under your wise leadership, any country represented here is making a contribution, it is because your government has created and continued to maintain those conditions which inspire and promote mutual co-operation, mutual interest and assure mutual benefits. The universality of the diplomatic representation near this Capital, therefore, attests the universality to the confidence which you and the people of your country have continued to enjoy among the nations and peoples of the world since your independence.

Finally Mr. President, permit me to say that the gesture, giving rise to this occasion comes from our human hearts; it is in spontaneous response to the many human kindnesses and the warmth of heart you have, from time to time shown, and out of which have grown the mutual esteem and friendship which increasingly continue to characterize our relationship.

8

AFRICA LIBERATION DAY

BROADCAST TO THE NATION

May 24, 1964

FRIENDS AND COUNTRYMEN,

A few hours from now, we shall be celebrating "Africa Liberation Day," marking the first anniversary of the signing, in Addis Ababa, of the historic Charter of the Organization of African Unity. This celebration will also mark our rededication to the struggle for the total liberation and Unity of Africa.

You will recall that the First Conference of Independent African States held in Accra in 1958 just one year after our independence, decided that the 15th of April will be "Africa Freedom Day." Now the Organization of African Unity has also decided that the anniversary of the signing of its Charter in May, 1963 shall be "Africa Liberation Day."

Africa Liberation Day therefore is now celebrated in all independent African States in remembrance of the epoch-making summit conference held last year in Addis Ababa when the Heads of Independent African States subscribed to the Charter of the Organization of African Unity.

In 1958, there were only eight independent African States. Today there are 33. Very shortly, this number will rise to 35 with the independence of Malawi and Zambia. There are still some 17 African territories to be liberated including South Africa, not mentioning some 25 Islands. We must now redouble our efforts to accelerate the liberation of these remaining territories in Africa.

We in Ghana are proud of the contribution we have made, materially, physically and morally to the liberation struggle. We shall continue to do so, because of our conviction that our own freedom and independence must depend on the total liberation and unity of Africa. On this occasion therefore we salute the gallant

47

freedom fighters who are actively engaged in the struggle for the liberation of territories in Africa not yet free and independent. We pay tribute to the memory of those who have fallen in the struggle.

I have spoken to you on many occasions about the tragedy in Angola and the other territories under Portuguese administration. Portugal continues to pursue a senseless and barbarous colonial war simply because it is haunted by the spectre of a past "Colonial Glory." Portugal refuses to accept the realities of the modern world and clings stubbornly to its inglorious colonial past. Portugal is an impoverished state hardly able to attend to the needs of its won population. It therefore uses a colonial war as a diversion of its people's minds from the sufferings at home. But Portugal can never win this war even with the support of powerful external forces. As a client state of the major NATO countries, Portugal has been able to obtain assistance from these countries to pursue its vicious policies in Angola, Mozambique and in other African territories under its domination. The ultimate responsibility for the continuance of this criminal and senseless colonial war, in which peaceful citizens including innocent children have been slaughtered, must rest at the door of the NATO countries.

In spite of the desperate stand of the Portuguese colonialists and their allies, the struggle for the total liberation of Africa continues with vigour. It is now time that we gave consideration to the means whereby the independence of the various liberated African States can be guaranteed.

As I have said time and time again, the salvation of Africa lies in Unity. Only a Union Government can safeguard the hard-won freedom of the various African States. Africa is rich, its resources are vast and yet African States are poor. It is only in a Union Government that we can find the capital to develop the immense economic resources of Africa.

Only a unified economic planning for development can give Africa the economic security essential for the prosperity and well-being of all its peoples.

It is also quite clear that not a single African State can today defend herself effectively. Therefore many African States are forced to enter defence agreements with their former colonial master. Recent events iŋ Gabon and elsewhere show clearly how these military Pacts can be used to subvert the independence and territorial integrity of African States. The only real and lasting solution is a defence arrangement for Africa on the basis of a unified military command.

We can go on to multiply the advantages of a Continental Union. Frontier problems disappear in a Continental Union. Irritating customs and other formalities cease to be barriers separating brother from brother. We can think of the great economic advantage of a common currency and a common market.

But all these can only be brought about by common aims and ideals under an effective political direction which can come only through a Union Government. That is why on the occasion of the first anniversary of Africa Liberation Day we should centre our thoughts on the establishment of a Union Government for Africa.

There is no time to waste. The longer we wait the stronger will be the hold on Africa by neo-colonialism and imperialism. A Union Government for Africa does not mean the loss of sovereignty by independent African States. A Union Government will rather strengthen the sovereignty of the individual states within the Union.

A year ago today saw the birth of the Organization of African Unity. Let us resolve on this first anniversary that the second meeting of the Heads of State of the Organization of African Unity in Cairo will see the birth of the Union Government of Africa.

9

THE PASSING OF
AN EMINENT STATESMAN

TRIBUTE ON THE DEATH OF
MR. PANDIT JAWAHARLAL NEHRU
PRIME MINISTER OF INDIA

May 27, 1964

GOOD EVENING,

Just before noon today, I received with profound distress the news of the sudden death of Prime Minister Nehru of India. I feel a sense of personal loss in the death of Mr. Nehru and I am sure that this is shared by you all in Ghana as well as millions in other parts of Africa and Asia.

Rarely have the qualities of wisdom, courage, humanity and great learning found such perfect fusion and expression in one individual, as they did in Pandit Nehru.

Soft of speech but forthright in expression, his voice was heard in the counsels of the world in defence of freedom and the dignity of man. He will long be remembered for his championship of the Afro-Asian cause and his support for the ideals of freedom, unity and world peace.

As a loyal apostle of Gandhi, Mr. Nehru showed wisdom and determination in carrying forward the great mission of welding the peoples of India into a united and progressive Nation.

His pre-occupation with the many problems of India did not prevent him from making the problems of other peoples his concern. His sympathy and understanding of the problems of Africa was a great source of encouragement to all of us who have been engaged in the struggle for the liberation and unity of Africa.

I recall the many occasions when I met Mr. Nehru at Commonwealth Prime Ministers' Conferences, at the United

Nations, and during my visit to India in 1959. On all these occasions, I was deeply impressed by his humanity, his wisdom, his vision and his profound understanding of our common problems and of the major issues of the world.

By Mr. Nehru's death the Commonwealth has lost a Prime Minister of outstanding courage and calibre. The people of India have lost a great and illustrious leader, and the world an eminent statesman.

On my own behalf and on behalf of the Government and People of Ghana I send to the Government and People of India my deepest condolence and sympathy. May he rest in peace.

10

THE CHALLENGE OF OUR SOCIALIST REVOLUTION

TO THE T.U.C. NATIONAL CONSULTATIVE CONFERENCE

Winneba
August 30, 1964

COMRADES,

On my own behalf and on behalf of the Central Committee of the Party, I send you warmest greetings on the occasion of the National Consultative Conference of the Trades Union Congress.

I am particularly happy that your Conference is taking place at a time when, more than at any time in our history, the working people of this country are being called upon to direct all their efforts towards the success of the Seven-Year Development Plan. This Plan is the greatest economic initiative in the entire history of our nation. Its significance lie in two facts. Through industrialisation and modernisation of agriculture, the Plan will put our economic independence on broad and secure foundations. In addition, the Plan is the first blueprint in the historic task of building a socialist society in this country.

Our Party has always served the working people of Ghana. Throughout its existence, the Party has honestly and doggedly fought to safeguard, protect and promote the interests of our workers. We have done all this because ours is the Party of the working people themselves. It has moved forward with the people. It has defended their interests honestly and selflessly. And it is but natural and logical that the Party should be recognised and acclaimed today as the leading force in the entire life of Ghana–the organiser, the educator and the guide of our people in all walks of life.

The prestige of our Party, is a clear demonstration of the confidence and hope our people repose in it. The mission which history has in.posed on us is that of ensuring our country's transformation into a socialist society, a society without the exploitation of man by man and in which man shall not be a wolf to his fellow man. There cannot be the slightest doubt that the Party, leading the nation and our entire working people, because of their confidence and support, will successfully fulfil this historic mission.

In building the economic and cultural foundations for a socialist society, our main task is to mobilise and direct all the forces and resources at our disposal towards the successful fulfilment of the Seven-Year Plan.

You meet at a time of great importance in our revolution. It was with you that we fought for the independence of this country. Now we must consolidate our gains in order to consummate our struggle for political freedom. We must, therefore, mobilise our efforts again in grand unison in order to ensure the success of our economic revolution. As I said when I launched the Seven-Year Development Plan, the success of the Plan will depend on the extent to which we can mobilise the enthusiasm of our workers so that they know the part they ought to play, and if they are drawn into full consultation in the execution of our Plan. I therefore call upon all workers, farmers, fishermen, and peasants of our country to accept this challenge and thus fulfil the hopes and aspirations of our people.

The basic task of our trade unions is to ensure that the targets set under the Plan are fulfilled and even over-fulfilled before schedule. I am glad to note that the workers have recognised this and are taking the necessary steps to ensure their active participation in the success of the Plan.

In embarking on socialist construction, our Party is fully aware that the success of the Plan depends to a decisive extent on our ability to draw out and unite the creative efforts of our people behind the Seven-Year Plan. I am happy that the trade unions are doing their utmost to revive the enthusiasm of our workers in order that our trade unions could fulfil their allotted tasks successfully.

Party guidance at all times and correct leadership of the Trades Union Congress are very essential if our trade union movements is to play a positive and decisive role in the present phase of our revolution. Our trade unions must carry out Party ideological education within the ranks of the workers in order to identify the masses even more closely with the activities of the Party. Every Party member must take an active part in organising and educating the people, in encouraging the initiative of the workers for the successful implementation of the Plan.

I have time and again emphasised that the conduct of all leading members in the various wings of the Party and in other high offices should be exemplary. I have, in particular, emphasised that bribery, corruption and nepotism are vices which we cannot tolerate, and that those who indulge in such practices will be discovered and ruthlessly smoked out from the Party and its integral wings.

Our socialist revolution demands that leading cadres of our Party be imbued with a sense of mission, selflessness, patriotism, devotion and dedication to our cause. The clean-up in the Trades Union Congress is a further assurance of the Party's determination to wipe out these social evils from our society. It should also serve as a warning to those who have not yet been discovered to rid themselves of such practices. More drastic steps will be taken in future against those who indulge in these malpractices.

This clean-up in the trade unions marks a new approach to trade unionism in this country. The present stage of our revolution calls for a new thinking and a new style of work in our trade unions. Our trade unions must move in line with our Party which is the supreme directing force behind our revolution. Our trade unions must eschew bureaucracy. They must be accountable to their rank and file and to the nation. And they must use some of their resources in providing educational facilities and welfare amenities for the workers. Without socialist morality and socialist consciousness we cannot achieve our socialist goals.

The responsibilities that the African revolution impose on our trade unions demand that we be exemplary in all our activities and that our public conduct be above reproach. The initiative of the African Revolution for achieving continental trade union unity has been placed in the hand of our workers. We must live up to expectation. We must never fail millions of workers and freedom fighters on our continent who look to us for inspiration and guidance.

The Party will continue as ever before to give active support to the trade unions. Together we shall lay a firm foundation for the construction of socialism and the fulfilment of the aims and aspirations of our people for a better life and happier future.

I wish your Conference every success.

11

PEACE AND PROGRESS

THE CONFERENCE OF NON-ALIGNED STATES

Cairo
October 7, 1964

MR. CHAIRMAN, DISTINGUISHED COLLEAGUES,

Three months ago, the Heads of State and Government of the independent African states met here in this ancient capital, and enjoyed the over-flowing hospitality of the people of Cairo. We met then—at the Summit Conference of the Organisation of African Unity—to forge new links of brotherhood and solidarity between our various states, and to take positive steps for the furtherance and consolidation of African Unity. Throughout our deliberations, we were deeply conscious of the sacredness of the task imposed upon us by destiny, and by our peoples; we were convinced that the unification of the African continent was a vital factor in the peace and security of the world.

On my own behalf and on behalf of the government and people of Ghana, I wish to join in expressing to President Nasser and the government and people of the United Arab Republic, our most sincere appreciation for offering yet again hospitality to another historic conference, and also for the courtesies which have been extended to us since our arrival here in Cairo.

Mr. Chairman, we, the representatives of the Non-Aligned States, are met here today to further our collective will and to consolidate our approach towards those problems which could trigger off another but a much more catastrophic war. We are all here as Non-Aligned nations but the term "Non-Aligned" as applied to us has not yet covered every form of policy which it connotes. We came into existence as a protest and a revolt against the state of affairs in international relations caused by the division of the world into opposing blocs of east and west. We came into existence as a revolt against imperialism and neo-colonialism which are also the basic causes of world tension and insecurity.

Mr. Chairman, we are meeting once more to concentrate our energies and our talents to the finding of ways and means, yes, to the finding of satisfactory and enduring solutions to some of the most difficult problems facing mankind today, the problems of peace, of the cold war, especially in the context of world—imperialism, of the elimination of military bases on the people's national territories, the problems of territorial and boundary dispute, the problems of imperialist and neo-colonialist intrigues and intervention. As we sit here, neo-colonialism has created a situation in Africa in which the only way it seems to fight and eradicate it is by armed revolution and armed struggle.

We, who are assembled here, represent the vast majority of mankind in Europe, Africa, Asia and Latin America, and from the borders and shores of the caribbean islands. Our peoples suffer most from the suffocating weight of the problems to which I have just referred. We must, therefore, accept boldly and fearlessly, the grave responsibility imposed upon us, at this Conference, of making such positive recommendations and decisions as will bring peace and tranquility to our people and to all mankind, realising that the destinies of millions of people are affected, not only of our generation, but of generations yet unborn.

At our first historic meeting in Belgrade, three years ago, we were drawn together by our common resolve that our view of the world situation, and our response to that situation should not conform necessarily, and as a matter of course, to the interests of either or the major power blocs. There were then 25 participating states and 3 observer countries. At this conference there are as many as 46 participating and 10 observer countries. This proves quite clearly that the policy of non-alignment, active and positive peaceful co-existence, the struggle against colonialism and the search for world peace have gained significant momentum. In Belgrade we recognised that the western bloc led by the United States of America, and the Eastern bloc led by the Soviet Union, because of their scientific and technological superiority, had acquired the means by which they could, by accident or by design, cause the destruction not only of themselves, but also of those of us who are non-aligned and who are in no way directly involved in their nuclear arms race. The main purpose of our meeting in Belgrade, therefore, was to use

57

all our exertions to influence the major powers, not only to abolish and destroy the nuclear stockpiles but also to divert into positive, progressive and constructive channels, the vast scientific and technological resources at their disposal for development purposes and for the peace, happiness and prosperity of mankind.

In some measure, we prevailed. We succeeded, and for the first time in human history, the great masses of the earth represented by the Heads of state and government present—forced the great powers to realise that to enter into nuclear war would be madness, and that no nation which pursued policies that might lead to such a war could count on the friendship of our peoples. We may here recall the historic commission which my friend the late Prime Minister Nehru and I undertook to Moscow, and a similar one undertaken by President Modibo Keita of Mali and President Sukarno of Indonesia to Washington. At this juncture, Mr. Chairman, I would like to pay tribute to the late Prime Minister Nehru, whose wise counsel we miss at this conference. With your indulgence, Mr. Chairman, I ask my colleagues to rise and observe a minute's silence in honour of Mr. Nehru.

Mr. Chairman, all of us here will agree that the dangers of a nuclear war today are considerably less than they were when we met in Belgrade three years ago. But we must face the fact that although the threat of war between the nuclear powers indeed seems somewhat to have diminished, owing to the balance of terror, most of the causes of tension in the world which we discussed are very much still with us today.

What are these major causes of tension in the world? It still remains true that the tensions which have produced the present uneasy world situation can be divided mainly into four classes. First, there are the tensions resulting from the problems left over from the Second World War. Foremost of these is the German issue, and the problem of Berlin which remains unsolved nearly nineteen years after the Second World War ended.

The German problem highlights the futility of modern war. This Conference is entitled to ask how long is the German issue going to be allowed to hang over the civilised world like the sword of democles? The West Germans talk of, and desire earnestly, the unity of Germany; the East Germans declare equally fervently their desire for German unity. Surely the time has come for a peaceful and early settlement of this thorny problem. In my view, this conference should call upon the two Germanies to come together to find a solution to the problem of German unity. Since, as non-aligned states, we have no interests; we should be prepared to put our good offices at their disposal.

Secondly, there are the tensions arising out of the striving of the peoples of the developing areas of the world to throw off their burdens of imperialism, colonialism, neo-colonialism and racial discrimination, in their efforts to create a better world for themselves without the interference, obstructions and interventions of foreign powers.

Thirdly, there are those divisions resulting from a conflict of ideologies. On this, may I say that just as there can be competing ideologies in the same society, so there can be opposing ideologies between different societies. However, while societies with different social systems can co-exist, their ideologies cannot. There is such a thing as peaceful co-existence between states with different social systems; but as long as oppressive classes exist, there can be no such hing as peaceful co-existence between opposing ideologies.

We cannot co-exist with imperialism, we cannot co-exist with colonialism; we cannot co-exist with neo-colonialism. There can never be co-existence between poverty and plenty, between the developing countries and the forces that militate against their progress and development.

Fourthly, there are tensions caused by the possession by the great powers of weapons, the destructive capacity of which there is no parallel in history.

To my mind, the overriding cause of tension in the world today lies in the second of the four classes of tension I have defined, namely the difficulties placed in the path of development of the emergent and developing nations by the imperialist and neo-colonialist powers. Thus we in Africa are threatened by two dangerous forces. The first is the desire of foreign powers to penetrate Africa, and establish new forms of colonialism through the vicious system of economic exploitation and economic imperialism. The world is witnessing the intrigues of this system in their classic form in the Congo and Southern Rhodesia.

The second threat to the new Africa is the danger of ultra-rightist trends in neo-colonialism, which I would designate as fascist imperialism. These trends are evident in certain quarters of the world today. They are not a flash in the pan. Nor do they represent the "Lunatic Fringe" of fascist imperialism. They are the political manifestation of a deadly evil which is capable of upsetting the peace of the world by turning the existing situation into a mad renewal of nuclear diplomacy.

Mr. Chairman, may I now turn hastily to the problem of the Congo which, as you know, continues to be torn by internal strife instigated and fomented by mercenaries and by foreign arms and intervention.

The malaise that has affected the very heart of Africa threatens to involve the future of the whole of our continent. It must be emphasized firmly here that African problems can be resolved best by Africans themselves. The Organisation of African Unity has shown by its efforts and record that it can, if let alone, solve African problems effectively.

It is imperative that a solution is found which will bring peace and harmony to the Congo. So long as the great powers continue to intervene in the affairs of the Congo, there will be no peace in the Congo or in Africa. This conference therefore should endorse the demand of the African people: Hands off the Congo, away with the mercenaries. The problem of the Congo, like all African problems, can only be solved by Africans themselves. My conviction is that the problem of the Congo is a political one and needs a political solution. I have suggested before that urgent consideration should be given to the following measures:—

(a) That the ad hoc commission of the Organisation of African Unity should see to it that the various political leaders and leaders of the warring factions should come together for national reconciliation and to make arrangements for the election of a democratic national government.

60

(b) In the meantime, there should be a cease-fire by both sides, and the Organisation of African Unity should provide a peace force to help maintain law and order until after the general election.

(c) That all foreign troops and mercenary soldiers should leave the Congo at once.

Mr. Chairman,

In South Africa and in Southern Rhodesia, a minority of European settlers, hoistered up by their powerful allies, are able to keep in subjugation the aspirations of the millions of Africans who form the majority, and to whom the land and its wealth belong. In the same way, Portugal supported by her NATO allies, is able to wage a savage war against the inhabitants of African territories several times larger than herself.

The minority regime in Southern Rhodesia clings blindly and stubbornly to a course which can only lead that unhappy nation down the road to violent revolution.

Mr. Chairman, as Non-Aligned states, we accept as a policy the general principle that territorial and boundary disputes should be settled without the use of force. We also accept that territorial and boundary disputes arising out of legacies of the colonial past of the newly independent and emerging countries of Asia and Africa and Latin America should by all means also be settled by peaceful negotiations. Agreed. But, Mr. Chairman, there are other territorial claims which arise out of imperialist and colonialist occupation. In this case the country occupied and victimised by a foreign power should have the right to use all means and resources at its disposal to recover its territory and safeguarded it. This is the basis of the liberation struggle in Africa.

And again, Mr. Chairman, we who claim to be non-aligned must have the right to choose the political and economic philosophy which we consider most suitable for our rapid development and advancement. For example, the fact that Ghana accepts socialism as a means of our political and economic development does not and should not place us in opposition to any other country or people. Socialism does not belong to the Soviet Union or to China, or for that matter to any other country; it is an international idea. Similarly, Capitalism does not belong to Britain, Western Germany or the United States of America. It is an economic doctrine and political philosophy which some of us consider unsuitable to our present circumstances. But this rejection of capitalist exploitation does not mean that we are politically opposed to the countries who have embraced capitalism. We are socialists. We are also non-aligned. We are opposed to political and economic exploitation and domination of man by man. We are against social injustice and inequality, against racism and racialism. We stand for progress, peace and justice.

Mr. Chairman, the fourth class of tension about which I spoke is the danger arising from the possession by the major powers of weapons of mass destruction. We have an opportunity at this conference, to take unequivocal stand on this issue. The arms race in which the so-called great powers are engaged must be stopped. It is not only dangerous to mankind; it is a senseless waste of national resources which should be diverted for the further development of large areas of the world, and the raising of the standards of living of the people of those areas. If a fraction of the millions being wasted on destructive nuclear weapons would be spent on atomic energy research, atomic energy could become as common as ordinary electricity. Imagine the effect which this contribution can have on the welfare and happiness of mankind. A policy based on the continuous threat of nuclear warfare, no less than nuclear warfare itself, is a policy of madness and despair, it is the clear duty of those of us here who profess to follow a positive non-aligned and neutralist policy to assert our full weight against such senseless policies. It is our duty also to express our surprise at the attitude of those nations who oppose the destruction of nuclear weapons. Let us declare to the world, here and now, that we demand complete and total disarmament.

Referring to the question of the elimination of foreign military bases in Africa, may I say, Mr. Chairman, that France's announcement of withdrawing her military bases from Africa is most welcome and should be vigorously implemented. We urge most strongly that this withdrawal should be complete and total. I hope all powers with military bases in Africa and elsewhere will do the same, and do it completely and totally.

Africa can only remain a nuclear free zone if the powers which now possess nuclear weapons divest themselves of these destructive nuclear weapons.

We are not and should not be a party to the cold war. It is not our conflict even though we suffer the consequences no less than those who are involved in the cold war. It is we who suffer the consequences of the cold war in Vietnam, Cyprus, Congo, Cuba, Laos and elsewhere. Our survival depends upon the ending of the cold war. Let us call upon the disarmament committee in Geneva to adopt a formula which will make possible the conclusion of an agreement for general and complete disarmament. We who are non-aligned should steer clear of all military blocs such as NATO, The Warsaw Pact, Cento and Seato, etc. etc.

Mr. Chairman, the 100 million dollars which is spent each hour of the 24 hours of the day on arms not only deprive the new emergent and developing countries of the essentials of life, but imposes upon them unnecessary difficulties and restrictions. The resources and money being wasted on such a frightening scale make it difficult for us to develop as rapidly as we can, because the resources that are essential for such development are used by the industrial powers not for peaceful purposes but for destruction. This inconceivable expenditure on arms, affects the policies of the developing countries of Asia, Africa, Latin America and elsewhere. Why should we be forced to spend money on armaments ? Why should we be forced to use oppressive methods and techniques to combat the great powers at intrigue and subversion.

It is quite clear that the question of development wherever it may be tackled, depends on total and complete world disarmament. We cannot develop until the arms race is ended. If the arms race is not ended our development will indeed be slow and our governments will be overthrown, and the crisis which is disturbing the world will multiply until we find ourselves in a final holocaust.

When the Afro-Asian states met in Bandung in 1955, we were able to produce the ten principles of co-existence and to establish Afro-Asian solidarity. It is imperative for the peace of the world that we should maintain and support the efforts of the Afro-Asian states at Bandung. In other words, the decisions taken here should support and reinforce the Bandung spirit.

Mr. Chairman, two further causes of tension in the world to which we must turn our attention are the need for the re-organisation of the United Nations, and the representation of China in the United Nations. In the view of Ghana, the most serious defect of the United Nations today is that its organisational structure has not kept pace with the changing realities of our time.

I must here refer to the continued absence of the People's Republic of China from her rightful seat at the United Nations. The absence of China from the United Nations has never made sense and will never make sense.

Peace in South-East Asia is vital to the peace of the world. The crisis that has arisen between Indonesia and Malaysia should therefore be resolved peacefully. In order to help Indonesia and Malaysia to settle their differences as brothers, this conference should lend its good offices through the medium of a mission or a conciliation Committee.

In Cyprus too, we face a problem which if not properly handled, could lead to a major struggle. The prerequisite to a solution of the Cyprus problem is that the independence and sovereignty of Cyprus should be respected and safeguarded so that the people of Cyprus may be in a position to find a democratic solution to their problems. Similarly, in the interests of world peace let us have peace and security in the Middle East.

Mr. Chairman, I will now state briefly the main points I wish to stress, and to indicate what I think this conference should attempt to achieve.

First, we should take up the challenge against imperialism, colonialism and neo-colonialism in all their forms and manifestations. Colonialism must end now. Let us give concrete expression to our hatred and abhorrence of these systems and expose their anachronism in the 20th century. Let us declare to the world that we are opposed to the political or economic domination of one people by another. To this end, we should, in accordance with the

64

United Nations Declaration on decolonisation, call upon the remaining colonial powers to grant independence without further delay to all territories now under their domination.

Secondly, we should ensure that the United Nations and its specialised Agencies are rapidly overhauled to reflect the new balance of forces in the world today.

Thirdly, we must consolidate and reinforce the solidarity achieved by the "77 Group" of developing countries at the Geneva Conference on World Trade and Development. In particular, we should call on the developed nations to adopt a new approach to world trade so as to make it possible for the developing countries to earn the means for financing their major development projects. Basically, what we want is trade, not aid.

Fourthly, as a major contribution to world peace, we must assist in ensuring that China is admitted to the United Nations this year. We should all pledge ourselves to the fulfilment of this objective.

Fifthly, the threat of nuclear warfare should be removed by our calling upon the nuclear powers to sign a treaty for total and complete disarmament. We should also ensure that the establishment of nuclear-free zones in the world is achieved as rapidly as possible. To this end, we must identify ourselves with efforts being made to secure total and complete disarmament.

Mr. Chairman, we live in a changing world. Out of the contradictions and conflicts of vested interests, a new inter- national community must emerge. The process may be slow, but it is inevitable and unmistakable. This new international community can only serve mankind if it is firmly established on freedom, equality, and inter-dependence among the nations.

It is in this context that the emergence of a revolutionary upsurge in Africa must be viewed. The African revolution represents a revolt against the inhuman exploitation and spoiliation of Africa and her people by foreign interests. The foundations of the new Africa are based, therefore, on complete emancipation from foreign domination: the political unification of all Africa and a determination to breathe the air of freedom which is theirs to breathe.

Mr. Chairman, throughout the world there is a deep seated but often inarticulate desire for peace, prosperity and progress. Let us help to make the progressive world opinion assert its full weight. In the modern world, every country is now a neighbouring country, owing to the great advances in scientific and technological achievement. It is thus the duty of all nations, big or small, weak or powerful, rich or poor, developed or deveLoping, to assist in ensuring to man, peace with himself and with the world. All our efforts here should contribute to the general cause of maintaining world peace against wars of aggression, against imperialism, against colonialism and neo-colonialism. The world is watching us, as we grapple with these problems. Let us accept the challenge honestly, incorruptibly, boldly and fearlessly.

12

AIR FORCE DAY

FIRST AIR FORCE DAY CELEBRATION

Takoradi
October 24, 1964

J am happy to be here with you today, for us to witness the Passing-out Parade of Officers on this first Air Force Day. I hope that this event will take place every year like we have it in the Army. And may such Passing-out Parade also be established for the Navy soon.

Such events will enable the people of Ghana to witness the work which our Armed Forces are doing in the country. The Armed Forces are the people's Armed Forces and the people must realise that it is their own. We have established these services out of scratch in order to protect the people and safeguard their interest and security. The Armed Forces are therefore the servants of the people. It is more so in a people's democracy. As you know, we have established a Military Academy and a higher Military College for the training of superior Army Officers. We are also laying the foundations for a Naval College and an Air Force College. The Gliding School that has been established at Afienya and which has a programme for making Ghanaians air-minded, and providing not only facilities for sport but also providing the necessary incentives for military and civil aviation, has made commendable progress. We hope to make it one of the best in the world and a model for all Africa.

May I now take the opportunity to congratulate those of you who have completed your training in our Air Force. Your graduation from this Centre, which we hope to develop into the Ghana Air Force College, is not the end of your endeavours but the beginning of a fascinating career. The conquest of space and the tremendous technological progress in aero-nautical science has made aircraft and aircraft design more and more sophisticating, requiring for their handling considerable alertness and presence of mind.

I am delighted to see two young women among those who are undergoing their training. May I extend my special congratulations to them and may their efforts serve as a growing symbol of the new womanhood of Ghana and of Independent United Africa. It may interest you to know that a Women's Military organisation is now being established within the Ghanaian Armed Forces to be known as the Women's Auxiliary Corps. It will be auxiliary to the Army, Navy and Air Force. This Women's Military Service will enable our young women to join in the Defence Services of the State and will enable them to move forward shoulder to shoulder with the men as they are already doing in many other fields of national activity.

The Ghana Air Force to which you who are graduating today belong, is a relatively young Service in Ghana. I inaugurated it barely 4 years ago in 1960 with the establishment here in Takoradi of the Air Force Training Centre. Since then progress and expansion of the Air Force have been steady and swift. I hope that this afternoon we shall see something of their efforts within this short period of time.

The major function of the Air Force is to assist the other services making up the Armed Forces to protect our frontiers and to safeguard territorial integrity. If a country is victimised by imperialism and occupied by a foreign power, if a country is subjected to the ravages of colonialism and neo-colonialism, then that country should have the right to use all the means at its disposal to recover its territory and defend its territorial integrity. This is the basis of our liberation struggle in Africa. This is the reason why Ghana is compelled to maintain an Army.

The Air Force has other duties as well; to give service to our people, and to make an effective contribution in every sphere of our national development. I recall that during the recent floods in the Northern and Volta Regions, the Air Force together with other military and civilian organisations played an important part in carrying essential supplies and foodstuffs to the affected areas in order to relieve the hardships of the people. Recently, the Air Force has been assigned the task of helping the Ministry of Health in the campaign for the eradication of malaria which is now proceeding nicely.

I have also directed that a scheme should be established for the use of Ghana Air Force planes in a Flying Doctor Service throughout the country. This will bring quick and efficient medical service to our people by linking the hospitals and medical centres throughout the country.

The Armed Forces have great responsibility to the Nation. This is why it is vital that its leadership should reflect and conform to the aspirations of the Party, the Government and the people. It must reflect the ideology of the African Revolution.

We now have our own Military Academy where Officers are trained for the three services of the Armed Forces. A new higher Military College has also been established at Teshie near Accra to train senior officers for higher military and administrative responsibility. As I have said, it is intended in the near future to establish a separate institution for the training of Military, Naval and Air Force Officers in greater numbers to prepare them for service within Ghana and elsewhere in Africa wherever they are needed.

The African revolution is unalterably opposed to imperialism, colonialism and neo-colonialism. To this end we are determined to achieve total victory. Africa must be free and united. It is the only basis on which we can assert and project the African personality, thus enabling Africa to play its full part within the world order for the peace, happiness and prosperity of mankind.

Recent events in Britain, the Soviet Union, China and other parts of the world seem to point unmistakably to the establishment of new dimensions and the creation of new problems in world affairs. The successful explosion of an atomic bomb by the Government of the People's Republic of China has been received with misgiving and disdain although we can understand and appreciate the point of view of the Chinese people in this great achievement. But a nuclear explosion by China must bring home to all of us the supreme danger facing mankind, the imperative necessity for peace and the urgent need for the establishment of general and complete disarmament. It is our hope that the nuclear powers, now including China, will make one more supreme effort for the attainment of complete and total disarmament and to seek to create the conditions for peace and world security.

As I have stated recently elsewhere, Africa cannot co-exist with imperialism; we cannot co-exist with colonialism; we cannot co-exist with neo-colonialism.. There can never be co-existence between poverty and plenty, between the developing countries and the forces that militate against their progress and development. We must therefore fight to conquer and destroy these anachronisms of our century.

We stand for peace; we stand for progress; we stand for justice. We look forward to the early establishment a of Continental Union Government of Africa which will throw the whole weight of a united Africa in support of peace and prosperity in the world.

Men and women of the Ghana Air Force, Ladies and Gentlemen, I wish once again to congratulate those officers who have obtained their Wings today, and also to say a word of thanks to the staff who have been responsible for the training in this Centre.

And now may I wish members of the Ghana Armed Forces success in their future endeavours.

Thank you.

UNDERSTANDING THE NEW AFRICA

THE SIXTEENTH ANNUAL NEW YEAR SCHOOL

Legon
December 28, 1964

On the occasion of the 16th Annual New Year School of the Institute of Public Education, 1 send my best wishes to the School.

I am happy to note that your theme for this year's school is "Understanding the New Africa." It is my view that Africa should produce a new African who not only recognises the dangers of imperialism, colonialism and neo-colonialism, but who is ever ready to stand resolutely against all the evils that depreciate the African Personality and hamper African progress and development.

Today, we see the naked manoeuvres of the neo-colonialists and the imperialists, in their intervention in the Congo, and in their calculated attempts to colonize Africa. If individual African States believe that they can stand on their own against this determined onslaught, then History has not really taught its lessons. Divided, Africa will revert to the era of colonial rule, but united under a Continental Union Government, Africa will develop into a mighty force and take her rightful place in the comity of nations. My message, therefore, to your School, to the youth of Ghana; and to the youth of Africa, is that we must unite now in Africa or perish.

I hope that you who are fortunate to be at this School will apply yourselves diligently to your studies and go back to your various walks of life, prepared to devote your energies to the service of Africa and the cause of its unity.

I wish your 16th Annual New Year School every success.

BRIGHT FUTURE FOR ALL

OPENING OF THE NATIONAL ASSEMBLY

January 12, 1965

MR. SPEAKER, MEMBERS AND COMRADES OF THE
NATIONAL ASSEMBLY,

J open this Fifth Session of Parliament at a time of great national expectation and promise. The implementation of our Seven-Year Development Plan which I launched a year ago, is proceeding vigorously. We have already exceeded during the first year of the Plan the investment target which we have set ourselves. This means that in terms of preparation and fulfilment for the future years of the Plan, we are already far ahead. We have laid a firm foundation for progress and sustained economic growth and expansion in the years ahead. I will say more about this later.

But the success of our national endeavours and our economic reconstruction depends on the maintenance of world peace. Ghana has played, and will continue to play, its part in the quest for peace within the comity of nations.

We cannot, however, ignore the fact that world peace depends on the attainment of total and complete disarmament. The stock-piling of nuclear weapons can only lead to tragic consequences for the world. No lasting peace can be achieved, until imperialism, colonialism and neo-colonialism, in all their forms and manifestations, have been abolished everywhere in the world. So long as imperialist and neo-colonialist intervention in other nations' affairs continues in any part of the world, world peace will continue to elude mankind.

The two greatest factors in the complicated society of the present century are decolonisation and automation. The attainment of complete decolonisation is a necessary condition for the proper distribution of historical initiative in society in order that everyone, every nation, every people, may attain their maximum development, and make a positive contribution towards world progress and civilisation.

Automation is the relationship between energy and human endurance, and should have for its aim the promotion of efficiency through the elimination of drudgery, and the enhancement of progress and development for all.

. Complete decolonisation, when linked with the development of automation to its highest possible limits, could well lead to a period of great progress and prosperity for mankind.

Barely three months ago in Cairo, 47 peace-loving nations, including Ghana, owing no allegiance to any of the power blocs into which our world is unhappily divided, solemnly re-affirmed their resolve and determination to reduce international tension and keep the world free from the threat and scourge of nuclear war. In order to prevent war and create conditions for peaceful development, the causes of war must be removed. The non-aligned nations therefore took an uncompromising stand against imperialism, colonialism and neo-colonialism—the major causes of international tension in the world to-day.

Mr. Speaker, the Cairo Summit Meetings of the Organisation of African Unity and of the Heads of State and Government of the non-aligned nations have strongly condemned the nuclear armament race and the proliferation of atomic weapons. But the danger of a further dissemination of nuclear arms has been growing within the past few months. And now what do we hear? There is talk among the NATO powers of a multilateral force. What is this multilateral force? What does it mean? It means the intensification of the cold war and the threat of a nuclear hot war. It also means the proliferation of nuclear weapons; in other words, more fingers on the nuclear trigger.

The Multilateral Force is to consist of twenty-five warships camouflaged as ordinary merchant freighters. These vessels are to be equipped with two-hundred and fifty death-dealing nuclear missiles of the "Polaris" type. The crew will be composed of two thousand NATO soldiers. This fleet is supposed to operate in the Atlantic Ocean and in the Mediterranean. That means that one day some neo-colonialist and imperialist warships can appear along the coast of Africa in order to assist the Portuguese colonialists in Angola, Mozambique and Portuguese Guinea in their fight against the liberation movement in Africa. For this reason, the Multilateral Nuclear Force is a dangerous threat not only to the peoples of Africa, but to world peace.

Therefore, the peoples of Africa and all anti-imperialist forces of the world who do not want to see themselves implicated in a new hot war, must raise their voices in protest against this dangerous development. The Multilateral Force is a naked contradiction of the Partial Test Ban Treaty.

We cannot convince any one that we sincerely seek peace by preparing for war. Peace can only be attained by acting peacefully and proscribing war in thought, word and deed. To this end, all the nations whose actions can lead to war on a world scale must begin now as a first step to prohibit the further manufacture of nuclear weapons. Putting a stop to the proliferation of nuclear weapons is, I repeat, only a first step in the process of making the world safe for peace. We must proceed to the next major step by agreeing to the total destruction of all such weapons throughout the world. If there are no more nuclear triggers around, we can be sure that there will be no fingers upon them. This is the surest way of making the world free from the threat of nuclear war.

Mr. Speaker, I am sure that effective and concerted action by the Independent African States and the peace-loving peoples of the world can ahd should destroy forever colonialism, imperialism and neo-colonialism. They are the forces of world tension.

The struggle against neo-colonialism and all its ramifications in Africa, is the struggle of all peoples—the workers and peasants of our continent.

My Government from the very dawn of independence committed and pledged Ghana and all her resources to the struggle for the total liberation and political unification of our continent. This titanic and arduous struggle, demands sacrifices from us all.

On various fields we have already scored some victories; the African trade unions are to-day united within the framework of the

All-African Trade Union Federation and are discovering for themselves the new philosophy of mutual co-operation between progressive national governments and the peoples' movements for the reconstruction of our national economy.

The trade union movement both in Ghana and in Africa has a very important role to play in the struggle to fight poverty, ignorance and disease, to help build new industries so to provide more employment facilities and thereby raise the standard of living of our growing population.

Here in Ghana, our Party as the vanguard Party of all sections of the community links closely together our trade unions and farmers organisations with the formulation and execution of Government policy. We call upon our workers to assume their full responsibility in all sectors of our industrial life and infuse into our working people the spirit of patriotism, love for one's country, which must help us increase productivity as the only way of increasing our national wealth.

When I addressed this House a year ago, I invited you to ratify the Charter of African Unity. The Organisation of African Unity has happily survived the border disputes between Ethiopia and Somalia, between Somalia and Kenya and between Algeria and Morocco.

The Organisation of African Unity has endorsed our positive stand on the Congo impasse, and asserted in no uncertain terms that the Congo problem demands a political solution. The Congo problem is not a military one. It is an African political issue. Mr. Speaker, wherever neo-colonialism operates, there is always trouble and confusion for the people in that area.

In September last year, I addressed a message to the Heads of States of the Independent African States in which I put forward the following proposals for dealing with the Congo problem, namely: the proclamation of a cease-fire forthwith, and neutralisation of all armies in the Congo. I proposed the summoning of a Round Table Conference of the leaders of all the main political parties and the revolutionary factions in the Congo to meet in Addis Ababa under the auspices of the Organisation of African Unity. This Conference is to agree to the setting up of a Provisional Government, with the sole object of organising a fair and peaceful general election under the auspices of the Organisation of African Unity.

I proposed furthermore that for the duration of the Round Table Conference and the general election, the Organisation of African Unity is to maintain a Peace Force in the Congo whose main responsibility is to assist the new Provisional Government with the preservation of law and order. This Peace Force is to be withdrawn as soon as the Round Table Conference and the general election have been concluded and a truly democratic government elected by the people established. These proposals were endorsed by the Council of Ministers of the Organisation of African Unity and I am happy to inform the House that the Security Council has recently passed a Resolution on the Congo which embodies our proposals.

There can be no peace in the Congo so long as foreign intervention and interference continues to hold sway and avenues for national reconciliation remain blocked and thwarted through neo-colonialist intrigues and pressures.

The compelling need now is for the establishment of a provisional Government of reconciliation composed of representatives of the main political parties to prepare the way for general elections under the auspices of the Organisation of African Unity. It would be difficult, ineffective and impracticable to organise O.A.U. forces on an ad hoc basis for peace keeping operations in the Congo and for the defence of the African Continent. That is why I have suggested that an all African Defence System or an African High Command be brought into being without delay. Such a Defence arrangement could be used to safeguard and protect the sovereignty of each African State, no matter how big or small.

If the Congo situation has not improved since I last addressed you, it is because those who oppose the legitimate and rightful aspirations of Africans in Angola, Mozambique, the so-called Portuguese Guinea, Southern Rhodesia and South Africa have acquired more strength and practical support from their imperialist and neo-colonialist allies. The situation would have been different if they had listened to us. We must warn the neo-colonialists and their agents that in spite of everything they do, the masses of Africa are awake, alert and on the march. The masses see through these intrigues and are determined to expose the enemies of Africa. History and time are on our side.

As I stressed in my address to you a year ago, the Addis Ababa Charter has already been overtaken by events. The Conference of African States in Cairo in July last year recognised this fact, and my call for a Union Government for Africa received at least the acknowledgement of my brother African Heads of State and Government. The study of Ghana's proposals for a Union Government was one of the main recommendations of the Cairo Conference.

Mr. Speaker, 1965 is a year of decision for Africa. The next Conference of the Organisation of African Unity will be held here in Accra this year. It is my earnest hope and expectation that this Conference will see the birth of a Continental Union Government for Africa. If we go fast we shall surely achieve success. If we go slow we shall go to pieces and perish.

Our efforts towards a Continental Union Government for Africa is only the first stage of our struggle to create the right image of Africa in the world, and to provide a secure political framework within which we can develop our natural resources and improve the standard of living of our peoples throughout the country.

Mr. Speaker, I referred earlier on in this address to the role which Ghana is playing in world affairs. To this end we have continued to fulfil our responsibilities to the United Nations. In spite of its imperfections, the United Nations is the surest guarantee of world peace. The House will be glad to know of the signal honour earned by Ghana and Africa by the appointment of our Permanent Representative in the United Nations, Mr. Alex Quaison-Sackey, as this year's President of the United Nations General Assembly.

With regard to the Commonwealth, we have played an active part in its deliberations, and have recently made suggestions for the setting up of a Commonwealth Secretariat which, when implemented, would make the Commonwealth a more positive force for progress and understanding.

Mr. Speaker, Members of the National Assembly: Let me now return to the domestic scene.

On the 11th of March last year, I presented to this House, our new Seven-Year Development Plan by means of which we seek to give effect to the Party's Programme of Work and Happiness. The Plan is designed to speed up the socialist transformation of our economy through rapid industrialisation and the diversification and modernisation of our agriculture.

A bold decision such as we have taken, to transform and modernise our economy based on the socialist exploitation and utilisation of our natural resources, calls for sacrifices.

The Seven-Year Development Plan is a blueprint for the first stage of our National reconstruction. Thanks to the far-sighted education and training programmes of our Party and Government, we have most of the trained personnel we need to help implement the Plan. We have been able to supplement our resources by employing technicians from friendly countries. What is required now is for us all to make sacrifices while we carry out our Programme. We need to make a strong national endeavour to save on consumption expenditure so as to enable us to divert more and more of our national wealth into productive investments. Already we have made considerable progress in this direction. We have succeeded in laying down a solid infrastructural base for our future industrial development, which is about the best in Africa. We have built a first-class network of roads, ports and communications. We have expanded our schools, colleges and universities to train our young people to man important positions in our national life. Very soon the Volta River Project will be generating electricity for our industries and homes.

This year we are embarking on the second annual programme of development under the Seven-Year Plan. This will involve a total expenditure of nearly eighty million Ghana pounds. The Annual Plan for 1965, of which I will give you more details presently, envisages the continued development of the nation on a broad front, but with the emphasis on the further expansion of agriculture, industry and education in accordance with the provisions of the Seven-Year Plan.

Our achievements in the past have been considerable, but there are certain aspects of our economic life about which I would like to

78

make a few remarks here. Some of these are beyond our control; others we can control and correct. Our external financial position, and especially our foreign exchange reserves position, have been a subject of uninformed comment from certain quarters of the foreign press recently.

The fact is that our efforts to develop and transform Ghana from an essentially agricultural country to a socialist industrialised State have been beset by an adverse turn in our terms of trade over the past five years. While, in actual volume, our exports—particularly of cocoa—have expanded considerably in recent years, there has been, during the same period, a disastrous fall in the world market price. When the cocoa crop was being ravaged by swollen shoot and cocoa was in short supply, the price went up, the manufacturers appealed to us to do what we could to increase supplies. We spent a lot of money to increase production. The result of our efforts has been that production has almost doubled, but the manufacturers and the speculators in the cocoa trade have taken advantage of this to depress the price of cocoa. That is why the Cocoa Producers' Alliance is taking positive action to improve the bargaining position of the producing countries. The Governments of the consuming and manufacturing countries have a responsibility in this matter and should take an active and positive interest in the issue. As a result of these adverse trends in the cocoa trade, our overall export earnings have failed to show a proportionate increase.

On the other hand, the need to press forward with our development programmes has resulted in an increase in imports, especially imports of machinery, plant and equipment from those very countries. The fall in our export earnings while our imports were increasing, has resulted in deficits in our balance of payments.

It is in order to arrest this drain on our foreign exchange reserves that we have had to establish the present system of import licensing and exchange control. Our principal aim is to conserve our foreign exchange resources. By doing this we shall be able to purchase the investment goods, such as factories, machinery, plant and equipment, which we need to produce a large portion of the goods required for local consumption.

In order fully to secure our economic independence, we must

79

invest in those basic industries which can make locally the machines and equipment we need for producing consumer goods in Ghana. Until we can make these machines here in Ghana, we shall continue to be economically dependent.

This is the reason why, for the time being, there will necessarily be shortages of the less essential consumer goods. It couldn't be otherwise. Government will nevertheless ensure that the essential ones are available in adequate quantities for the people. This means that we have taken a stand to extricate ourselves from the economic shackles inherited from our colonial past. Don't forget that we are at war with neo-colonialism.

The Government is seriously concerned about the shortages of some essential commodities that developed during the latter part of 1964. We have therefore instituted appropriate measures to eliminate such shortages. Steps have been taken to ensure the smooth working of the licensing procedure, so as to avoid any bottlenecks which might hamper our industrial production and slow down our economic activity.

Mr. Speaker, as you can see around you everywhere, the Government has embarked on a gigantic programme of reconstruction. This programme of reconstruction has led to increased employment all over the country. As a result, money incomes and currency in circulation have increased considerably in recent years. This means that the purchasing power of our people has increased over the past years. But, as I have said before, our. programme of development and industrialisation demand that we should—for the time being—restrict imports and cut down consumption expenditure, particularly on luxury items. This process of restricting imports, at the same time that the money in the hands of the people is on the increase, has led to a pressure of demand on the economy. In other words, there is more money chasing fewer goods. Prices therefore tended to rise and some retail traders found an easy means of getting rich quickly by exploiting the situation, indulging in blackmarketing and profiteering, and charging exhorbitant prices.

Unfortunately, some retailers have been known to have held back stocks in order to force prices up further. Individuals too on the other hand, have tried to hedge themselves against any possible price rises by hoarding stocks of consumer goods for future use. In other words, some traders and a few individuals are now indulging in speculation and profiteering at the expense of the broad masses of the people. This unpatriotic behaviour cannot be permitted to continue unchecked, and appropriate steps have been taken.

Let us be quite clear about the need for a system of controls during this period of reconstruction. The controls are necessary as a basis for our industrialisation programme, in order to cut down wasteful expenditure on luxuries and direct our resources to investment expenditure. The controls are essential if we are to conserve foreign exchange resources to finance imports of machinery, plant and equipment for our factories, which are going to produce the goods. By means of these controls, we are able to protect our local industries and create an effective market for their products.

And here, Mr. Speaker, may I congratulate our people and express appreciation for their understanding and co-operation in these matters. When we explain to them they understand. I have directed that the system of price controls should be strengthened, and everything possible is being done to check the current practice of profiteering and black-marketing. The Party and the Government take a very serious view of this.

While our people accept the need of self-denial and thrift, we must encourage them by showing results at home. On the infrastructural and construction projects there is no doubt that we have an impressive record of achievement. What is needed now is that our State Farms, the United Ghana Farmers Council Co-operatives and the State-owned and joint enterprises should produce, in sufficient quantities, and at reasonable prices, the commodities we require to meet the pressure of demand at home.

Mr. Speaker, I have had occasion before to mention to the House that our State enterprises—and this includes the State Farms and the Agricultural wing of the Workers Brigade—were not set up to lose money. The number of State Corporations which have been established has been determined by our policy of socialist construction and the building up of a socialist economy in Ghana. But the State enterprises, like any other enterprise, have a duty to operate on profitable basis, and thereby earn sufficient returns on the initial capital invested by Government. Those in charge of the State enterprises must realise that the investments in the factories with which they are entrusted, are financed from the hard-earned savings of the individual tax payer! The management and the workers in our State Farms and State Enterprises must realise that they have been entrusted with the management of vital economic units on behalf of the people, and the Party and the Government expect reasonable returns on these investments.

State Enterprises are the main economic pillars on which we expect to build our socialist State. We will continue to expand the public sector of the economy by establishing more State-owned enterprises both in industry and in agriculture.

The cocoa processing plants at Takoradi and Tema, the Steelworks Corporation which will be responsible for all iron and steel works in Ghana, the glass factory at Abosso, which is soon to go into operation, a meat processing plant in Bolgatanga, a textile mill, a radio and television Assembly Plant and a Cement Works at Tema, these are a few. All these are soon to go into operation. We also hope to transform a number of Government Departments like the railway, transport, electricity and printing into Corporations.

We have at present 35 State Enterprises in operation and additional new ones are being established right now which will bring the total to 60.

In addition to these State Enterprises, Government has shareholding in nine joint enterprises. Discussions are at present proceeding which will add three more enterprises to the list of Joint Enterprises to bring the number to twelve. The State Enterprises Secretariat will represent Government on the Boards of these Joint Enterprises and ensure that the interests of Government are fully safeguarded.

Ministers will be assigned responsibility for these Corporations, and will be responsible for them in Parliament, but the State Enterprises Secretariat, which is under the Presidency, will have the overall responsibility for ensuring that these Corporations are run efficiently and profitably, and in accordance with the terms of their instruments of incorporation.

In view of the special requirements for the staffing and organisation of State enterprises, a special procedure will be established for the recruitment, training and discipline of staff of all State enterprises. The employees of these State enterprises will be removed from the control of the Civil Service Commission and the Civil Service Regulations and Procedures.

In accordance with the Instruments of Incorporation under which the State Corporations are being set up, appointments to the Corporations will be made by the Boards of these Corporations. The State Enterprises Secretariat will, however, ensure that these appointments are proper and that the salary scales fixed for them fit into the general pattern of salaries and working conditions which is being worked out for State Enterprises. Appointments to positions of Manager and comparable posts will be made by the Minister with the approval of the Cabinet and upon the recommendations of the State Enterprises Secretariat.

A sharp distinction will be made, in this connection, between the Civil Service, the members of which are governed by the Civil Service Act, and the Public Service, which will embrace those other officers of the State including employees of State enterprises not governed by the Civil Service Act and the Regulations under it. Steps are being taken to merge the Civil Service Commission and the Establishment Secretariat in the interest of efficiency.

The aim of the Party and Government is to make our State enterprises efficient and profitable State organisations, and to run them on sound commercial lines. Every effort will be made to set them production and financial targets, and their profits will be paid to the State revenue to enable the Government to help finance its industrial and agricultural projects.

Mr. Speaker, if you allow me I shall now turn to matters relating to our fiscal and monetary policy for 1965. Members of the House know that we have recently been running budget deficits of varying levels. This is essentially because of the sharp fall in the price of cocoa which apart from being our main foreign exchange earner, is for the time being, that is to say until we have diversified our agriculture, one of the main sources of revenue by way of export duty. As you know, the export duty on cocoa is worked on a sliding scale so that the higher the price the more the revenue accruing to Government. The fall in cocoa prices, therefore, has meant a serious short fall in revenue. Hitherto, we have managed to finance our development expenditure by borrowing both from our own internal sources and from abroad. But as I have pointed out earlier, our programme of rapid development has resulted in considerable increase in money circulation. It has therefore become necessary to divert the weight of our development expenditure in the coming years from non-productive to directly productive investments.

The creation of heavy industry with the simultaneous growth of light industry and agriculture will be given priority in our industrial development. This can create the backbone of our national economy and lay solidly the foundations of our socialist industrialisation.

Our heavy industries should comprise power industry, metallurgical industry, machine building industry, chemical industry, building material industry, alumina industry, iron and steel industry, and so forth. Such industries directly related to the living conditions and requirements of the people will provide the machinery for producing food, clothing and housing. It is in this way that our heavy industry can be made to serve more effectively light industry and agriculture.

In order to provide the necessary support for the many industrial and other projects now springing up throughout the country, the Government has already made plans for the establishment of heavy basic industries for the production of the machine tools and industrial equipment for our primary and light industries. This aspect of the Seven-Year Development Plan will now be given special emphasis in the remaining years of the Plan. Unless we can do this, our local industries will continue, for many years to come, to rely on foreign supplies for the renewal of their spare parts and equipment. Real industrialisation can only be achieved when we have embarked upon, and completed a programme of establishing heavy industries.

This cannot be achieved overnight. Our policy over the coming years will therefore be guided by the following principles: Firstly, an attempt will be made to close the budgetary gap while at the same time shifting the weight of development expenditure to productive investments in agriculture and industry. For this reason I have directed that the overall size of the Budget for 1965 should not exceed two hundred million Ghana pounds. This is the highest ever in Ghana. This will allow sufficient funds to continue work on existing projects as well as for starting a few new ones.

We could easily and usefully provide a budget for additional productive products in the course of the year which would bring our expenditure ceiling to two hundred and fifty million, if additional external credits can be obtained to finance these new projects. In other words, our present overall ceiling of two hundred million will only be exceeded if additional credits are obtained. In this regard, our policy is that new credits should now be confined mainly to productive investments in agriculture and industry.

Secondly, the Budget Estimates for 1965 will be broken down into foreign and local currency components. In the past, the estimates have been restricted only to cash expenditure. Credit-financed expenditure was excluded from the estimates on the assumption that it did not involve direct or immediate disbursements. Although this assumption is correct, the effect of this practice of excluding credit-financed expenditure from the estimates has been to understate the true size of the Budget. The 1965 Budget Estimates will now for the first time, show the total estimated expenditure during the year, indicating which project is to be financed on cash and how much on credit basis.

A third new feature of the 1965 Budget will be the presentation to Parliament for the first time of an Export and Import Plan and a Foreign Exchange Budget. I have already mentioned that the requirements of our development programme are such that we must conserve every possible source of foreign exchange for imports of investment goods. In order to do this effectively we have to plan our foreign exchange expenditure carefully during the year. I have accordingly directed the Minister of Finance to take the necessary steps to achieve this.

The fourth new feature of the 1965 Budget will be the presentation for the first time of a brief analysis of the latest balance sheets of each of our State-owned and Joint enterprises together with their financial plans and output targets. This will enable the Members of the House to see clearly for themselves the progress and development made by these institutions.

And now, Mr. Speaker, may I now touch briefly on the broad outline of our fiscal policy for 1965. The first years of budgetary practice and fiscal policy since independence were the formative years. During that period, our policy was aimed at laying the foundations of a broadly based tax structure which will enable us to increase revenue to meet our development expenditure. We have now reached a stage where certain refinements will be necessary in the tax structure. The Minister of Finance will announce the details in his Budget Statement. In addition to these adjustments, the system of collection of existing taxes will be improved and strengthened to reduce the possibility of evasion.

In this connection, and in view of our pressing need for foreign exchange, I want to take this opportunity to appeal to all patriotic Ghanaians who have funds abroad to make these funds available to the nation for the purchase of investment goods for our economic development. It has come to my notice that for fear that their bank balances at home might swell up unduly and cause embarrassment, those both inside and outside this House who have funds abroad, have been reluctant to repatriate their savings. In order to overcome their fears, I advise them to invest in the Bearer Bonds which were recently issued by the Bank of Ghana. Anyone with savings abroad may buy Bearer Bonds from Ghana Commercial Bank or any of its agents abroad. Since the Bonds do not bear any names, the identity of the holder can remain unknown until maturity if the holder so chooses. By buying the Bonds with his foreign currency savings, the holder would have done a useful service to Ghana. I therefore appeal to all of you who have funds abroad to seize this opportunity and show your patriotic spirit by using your foreign savings to take up our Bearer Bonds.

May I interpolate here: as the House is aware, preparations have been proceeding in the past few years for the introduction of a decimal system of currency. The new currency will come into use in July this year, so study its implications now. In line with the Government's intention to introduce a decimal currency, it is proposed to adopt the metric system of measurement which is simple and more universal.

Mr. Speaker, I shall now give the House some insight into our plans for 1965. I have already stated that we intend during the rest of the plan period, to shift the weight of our development expenditure in favour of the economic services. Agriculture is one of the basic starting points of any programme of industrialisation. For the tasks ahead of us, we must ensure that there is an abundance of food at cheap prices for·our people. For this reason, we shall press forward with our programme of rapid development, mechanisation and diversification of our agriculture. Such efforts will be supported by efficient systems of food storage and distribution. In this way, we shall be able in a short period of time to stabilise food prices.

One of the problems which has plagued our farmers over the years is lack of capital. The Commercial Banks, because of the large element of risk involved in agricultural production, do not readily invest in agricultural projects. Therefore, the farmers are forced to borrow from unscrupulous moneylenders who charge them exorbitant rates of interest. In some cases the interest payments are so heavy that the farmers are unable to meet their obligations to their creditors and eventually lose their farms. For this reason, we have decided to establish an Agricultural Credit and Co-operative Bank. A Bill for this will be introduced by the Minister of Finance during the early part of this session.

And here again our farmers have set us another example of public spirit and foresight by a voluntary decision on their part to subscribe four shillings for every load of cocoa as a Trust Fund to finance the Agricultural Bank. This Fund will be earmarked in the Bank to be used for granting loans at cheap rates of interest to the farmers themselves for the development of their farms as and when they need such financial assistance. As practical economists, our farmers have realised that this provision will help to reduce the pressure of demand on the economy. This they know will result in a lowering of prices of the goods which they require for their daily needs. And here again, Members of the National Assembly, I say "Hats off to our farmers!"

Now, returning to our industrial programme, we have continued to lay the basic foundations for the evolution of a socialist industrialisation based on efficient and rational methods of production. In 1963 our total investment in plant and machinery amounted to twenty-two million Ghana pounds and for the first time, industry accounted for more than twenty per cent of gross domestic investment in Ghana.

Our development estimates for this year provide for an additional expenditure of twenty million pounds for new investment in the State sector of industry alone. This does not include our annual contribution of seven million towards the Volta River Project. Let me say by way of parenthesis that the work on the main Volta Dam will be completed in a few weeks time, and it is expected that electric power from the Volta will be available by September this year.

As the construction of the Volta River Project draws to a close, the large labour force which it has attracted will be progressively diverted into other gainful forms of employment, such as the work on the construction of the smelter at Tema as well as the industrial complexes which we have already planned for the industrial development of the country.

Mr. Speaker, I have recently cut the sod for work to start on the Smelter at Tema. This Smelter will provide initially the largest market for the electricity to be produced from the Volta River Dam.

With the political stability and excellent infrastructure that our country offers, together with the abundant supply of electric power which will soon be available, Ghana offers as good investmen possibilities as you can find anywhere in the world. The Capital Investments Board will, this year, intensify its activities to stimulate foreign investment in Ghana. Several private investors and financiers are at the moment negotiating with Government bodies for the construction and operation of various other industrial projects in Ghana.

Mr. Speaker, Members of the National Assembly: While concentrating our attention on the expansion of our economy, we are not neglecting the development of our social services. Ghana is dedicated to the policy of free Primary Education. Already we have well over one million children in Primary Schools alone. Our free primary education system continues to expand at a fast rate. By the end of the current Plan period in 1970, over one million more—that is, two million children—will have been enrolled in our free Primary Schools.

To meet this vastly accelerated increase, the Seven-Year Development Plan provides for the inauguration of a new crash programme aimed at increasing the supply of trained teachers. This programme envisages the development of nearly fifty Teacher-Training Colleges into three-stream institutions each with a student population of about 500, and the construction of ten new Teacher Training Colleges and Institutions for the training of specialist teachers.

This academic year, over 8,000 new students entered our Secondary and Technical Institutions. It is our determination to lay a firm foundation now for universal free Secondary and Technical education in Ghana. To this end we are expanding the facilities for Secondary and Technical education.

Mr. Speaker, I am happy to announce that with effect from September this year, when the new academic year starts, Secondary and Technical education in Ghana will be completely fee-free. This will mark a great milestone in our educational advancement. But, Mr. Speaker, I want the House to know that at the moment our budget for education is the largest single item in our educational expenditure.

Reforms have already been introduced to encourage students in our Primary, Middle and Secondary Schools to combine academic work with the acquisition of basic technical skills for the manpower requirements of industry, commerce and agriculture. In addition, arrangements have been made for the teaching of typing, book-keeping and accountancy in all our Secondary Schools. The educational system as a whole will be re-orientated to meet the requirements of our African environment and our socialist programme. In other words, African History, African Law, African Literature and Folk-lore, as well as Ghanaian languages will be taught side by side with Arabic, French, English and Swahili in our Secondary Schools. The Institute of Languages is fitted with the

89

latest equipment for language instruction, and is doing a good job. Some of you must go to that school. New school syllabuses have already been introduced to give effect to our policy decision in these matters.

Mr. Speaker, you will be happy to know that enrolment in our universities has increased from 2,500 in 1964 to 3,480 this year. A further expansion is planned. Construction work on the necessary physical requirements for this expansion has already started. Our plan target is to increase enrolment of regular students in university institutions to about 25,000 by 1970. University education in Ghana is free and will continue to be free. It will be accessible to all who are capable of higher learning.

To avoid wasteful duplication in our universities and to harness effectively all our manpower, laboratory and other resources for the task of producing suitably qualified graduates, we have re-defined the functions of each of our existing three university institutions and assigned specific areas of study to them.

The University College of Science Education at Cape Coast will be responsible for the training and production of professional and graduate science teachers who are required to teach in our Secondary Schools and Polytechnics. In order to make the University College of Science Education the National Centre for research and teaching in education, our Government has also decided that the Institute and Department of Education at the University of Ghana and the Science Research Unit of the Kwame Nkrumah University of Science and Technology should be transferred to Cape Coast.

The Kwame Nkrumah University of Science and Technology will henceforth confine its degree courses to engineering, applied science and technology.

The University of Ghana has been assigned the responsibility for running degree courses in pure Science and in the Arts and the Humanities. To achieve this aim, the degree courses in Science and Arts previously run in Kumasi and Cape Coast have been transferred to the University of Ghana.

In order to increase student numbers in our Universities, all our universities have opened their doors to non-resident students since the beginning of the last academic year. This is another revolutionary advance in our higher education system.

As I have said before, agriculture is the bulwark of Ghana's national economy and the basis of our socialist industrialisation. It is important, therefore, that high priority be accorded to Agricultural Education. The Government has decided, therefore, to establish a University College of Agriculture which will take over, co-ordinate and develop the teaching and research in Agriculture now being undertaken at the University of Ghana and the Kwame Nkrumah University of Science and Technology and other Agricultural Research Centres in the country.

Mr. Speaker, a thorough review has been made of the new role which science and scientific research should play in our national development. The Ghana Academy of Sciences and the Institutes under it have been completely re-organised. In order to meet present and future needs of the country, 18 new scientific Institutes will be established under the Ghana Academy of Sciences. Already there are seven Institutes under the Academy, namely: the Building and Road Research Institute; the Forest Products Research Institute; the Crop Research Institute; the Cocoa Research Institute; the Animal Research Institute; the Soil Research Institute and the Institute of Health and Medical Research. The new institutes which are planned include: an Institute of Nuclear Research; an Institute of Aquatic Biology and an Institute of Wild Life Management.

Each institute under the Academy of Sciences will be autonomous under its Director as regards the execution of his work and programme as approved by the Praesidium and will be free to initiate new research projects such as will benefit the country.

In accordance with our policy of encouraging training in science and technology, and in order to fulfil Ghana's economic and industrial programmes, a special scholarship scheme will be implemented for students in science, engineering, medicine and technology. As from the next academic year, an increased scholarship allowance will be paid to all science students in our universities and also to pre-medical students.

Post graduate students in science studying at the three universities will also be given an increased scholarship allowance. A special State Fund will be created out of which loans will be given for post graduate and professional courses and subjects other than science.

Mr. Speaker, turning to our Housing programme we must have a place to sleep. As part of our social services for our people, Government will embark this year on major housing projects throughout the country. The concrete prefabricated Housing Factory which is now being built, will begin production in June this year and will help in accelerating our housing programme.

Mr. Speaker, some time ago, the Romans said: *Mens sana in corpore sano.* The health needs of the people will continue to receive the urgent attention of my Government.

Our aim is to provide free health facilities for the entire population of Ghana by the end of the Seven-Year Development Plan period. We shall, in this connection, extend rural medical services and intensify the training of medical and para-medical personnel to cope with the rapid expansion envisaged in the Plan.

For the accelerated training of doctors, in addition to nearly one thousand students receiving medical training on scholarships abroad, we have on our own initiative established a Medical School at Korle Bu and already 82 medical students are being trained in our own institutions in Ghana. The Medical School has been established as an autonomous institution, and will in due course develop a special relationship with the University of Ghana.

The training of doctors in the Medical School will take not less than seven years, arranged as follows: one year for pre-medical training; two years for pre-clinical training followed by three years clinical work and training. At the end of this period, students of the Medical School will qualify for the M. B. Degree. They will not be registered to practise as doctors, however, until they have completed one year's compulsory internship or housemanship after qualification. After registration as doctors at the end of the seventh year, they will be required to undertake a second year's internship in order to qualify to practise completely on their own. They will then be eligible for the award of the M.D. Degree on the submission of an approved thesis.

Care has thus been taken to ensure that the graduates of the Medical School will compare with the best from leading medical institutions in any part of the world.

As a means of reinforcing the facilities for medical training and research, it is intended, this year, to start work on a Medical Centre comprising a Teaching Hospital, Nursing Training School, Dental School and Post-Graduate Institution for Doctors and Scientists.

Mr. Speaker, the latest addition to our modern media of Communication is television. Ghana television will begin operation sometime this year.

Our television will be utilized not for cheap entertainment or commercialism, but for the furthering of our socialist ideals and the enhancement of our educational programme. It will also provide stimulating experience and relaxation.

Special training institutions are being established for the training of television personnel and the training of teachers in the use of television for science education.

In order to ensure that the benefits of television are extended throughout Ghana a new Transmission Station has been established at Tamale, in addition to the Station in Accra.

Mr. Speaker, Members of the National Assembly: As a further mark of the Party's determination to provide our workers with social security and welfare facilities during their working life and in their retirement, the Social Security Bill will come before the House this session. This Bill is the first practical step towards removing from our society the hazards and difficulties that attend retirement and old age, and is the foundation for a comprehensive Social Security Scheme for the people of Ghana. This is another revolutionary step in our socialist programme.

Mr. Speaker, the Party and the Government hold firmly to the belief that within our lifetime, the living conditions of our people can be radically improved and the standard considerably raised. If we are to succeed, our development projects must be executed with realism and with a sense of mission. One heavy drain on our resources is the unreasonably high cost of construction in Ghana. The Party and the Government is therefore determined to reduce construction costs. The Government's tender procedure has been revised to ensure that contractors provide a breakdown of each contract price into labour costs, the cost of materials, over-head costs, and the profit element. In this break-down, the foreign exchange as well as the local currency components will also be clearly laid down. No contractor will be awarded any further contracts until he can show clearly that he has paid his Income Tax to the full. All contracts involving the payment of foreign exchange must continue to be channelled through the Contracts Committee whose prior approval will be necessary before any contract is signed.

Mr. Speaker, I want to say a few words about our Armed Forces. We wish we did not have to spend much on defence since we believe that there are other ways of solving national and international issues other than resort to war.

The role of our Armed Forces continues to be: to defend the territorial integrity of Ghana in any case from external aggression and internal subversion, and to assist in ensuring the security of the African continent within the context of the Charter of the Organisation of African Unity. But to us the most important role of our Armed Forces is to assist in the execution of projects of national development.

The Armed Forces provide a valuable reservoir of skilled and highly disciplined man-power and it is our intention to have this man-power fully utilized for achieving the aims of the Seven-Year Development Plan. The major aspects of this contribution are to provide industrial training of soldiers in order to increase the technical potential available to the country; and to render increased assistance in the construction of roads and building projects. For this purpose, a special construction unit of the Army Engineers has now been established. This unit will devote itself exclusively to the execution of development projects.

In the same spirit, the Ghana Air Force is already engaged in

94

anti-malaria aerial spraying, and in aerial surveys for planned development projects. It has been used in the movement of essential supplies within Ghana to areas afflicted by floods and has already made a beginning in the establishment of a Flying Doctor Service. At the moment, some of our women are undergoing Pilot Training at the Ghana Air Force Training School at Takoradi.

Our Navy too is increasing in strength and has expanded its training programme to provide skilled technicians for our mercantile marine and our fishing fleet.

We have also established a Women's Auxiliary Corps which will enable our young women to work together shoulder to shoulder with the men in the service and development of our country.

Mr. Speaker, I intend to announce shortly a re-organisation of Ministries and Departments, the object of which is to increase the efficiency of the public service.

Finally, Mr. Speaker, Article 23 of the Constitution of the Republic requires that the National Assembly should be dissolved on the expiration of five years from its first sitting. Under the Constitution Consequential Provisions Act, 1960, the first sitting of the National Assembly was with effect from 1st July, 1960. It follows therefore that a General Election of new Members must be held before 1st July, 1965. Arrangements have been made accordingly.

As you know, the Delimitation Commission which considered the question of Electoral Districts has recommended certain inter-regional border adjustments. The Commission's recommendations are receiving the attention of the Government.

Our new Parliament will be enlarged, and will continue to be a forum for the expression of views fully reflecting the spirit of our socialist revolution and of the new age in Africa. Mr. Speaker, judging from the increasingly enthusiastic manner in which Positive Action Day has been celebrated throughout the country, it is clear that January 8th has become one of the most enduring and significant symbols of our national struggle for independence. Positive Action Day is significant, not only as a symbol of Ghana's struggle for independence; it also marks a great turning point in the struggle for Africa's liberation. It is the spirit of Positive Action that set in motion the liberation movement in Africa. Ghana will, therefore, continue to give maximum support and assistance to the freedom fighters and liberation movements in Africa for the final and total liquidation of imperialism and colonialism from Africa.

In order to keep alive the spirit of Positive Action, and to remind us of our responsibilities to Ghana and to Africa, I have directed that as from next year, Positive Action Day will be observed as a Public Holiday.

Mr. Speaker, Members and Comrades of the National Assembly: As I said at the beginning of this address, 1965 is a year of great expectation and promise. Let us therefore match our will and determination to the great responsibility that lies ahead. With unity, co-operation and mutual understanding we shall see the glorious fulfilment of our hopes and aspirations. As our cause is just and as our endeavours are geared to the well-being and happiness of all, let us march forward together determined to establish in our time a strong, prosperous and industrialised nation striving after the pursuits of peace in service to Africa and mankind.

I now leave you to your deliberations and pray that you be guided by the highest interest of the Nation.

15

THE OSAGYEFO PLAYERS

INAUGURATION OF "THE OSAGYEFO PLAYERS"

Flagstaff House
January 24, 1965

J have asked you to come here this evening for a very special and, to me, important reason. I know that all of you are interested in art, music and drama. In fact you are all keen students of drama and have taken leading parts in many plays in this country.

I have therefore brought you together to form this drama group, so that by the quality of your performances you will provide the intellectual and artistic stimulus for art and drama in Ghana.

We have in Ghana and in Africa a rich cultural heritage in art, music, drama, paintings and sculpture which colonialism sought in vain to destroy. Our culture and traditions have survived because they possess a special in-born power, a peculiar cultural image which we must now take upon ourselves to cultivate and develop. What we are about to set up now—and that is why you are here—must therefore rest in a healthy and dynamic expression of African genius and creative power. African Art and Epos are bound up with the forms of our social and cultural development.

As you know, I have initiated the establishment of the Institute of Art and Culture, the Institute of African Studies, and the School of Music and Drama at Legon. We also hope to launch a film and television school for training producers and artistes. We already have a Ghana Symphony Orchestra and a Choir which are showing great promise. All these institutions and this drama group which we are initiating today mark a forward step in the development of the Arts in Ghana.

I know that you are all fully employed and that you should not let your activities in this drama group interfere with it. It is my hope, however, that each one of you in this group will bring into it all your dramatic talents and experience, artistry and vigour. Here we shall work together and exchange ideas, and out of this activity we shall contribute to the progress of the theatre movement in Ghana. In other words, I look upon this drama group to be the intellectual centre, artistic stimulus and driving force behind the theatre movement in Ghana and the cultural renaissance of Africa.

It is only when there is complete fusion between African culture and African politics that the African Personality will find its highest expression.

I now, friends and comrades in the Arts, have great pleasure in inaugurating THE OSAGYEFO PLAYERS.

16

CHALLENGE TO OUR SURVIVAL

National Assembly
March 26, 1965

MR. SPEAKER, MEMBERS AND COMRADES OF THE
NATIONAL ASSEMBLY,

Four days ago, I addressed this house on the grave dangers facing Africa and exposed the crimes against the people of our continent, particularly in the Congo. I spoke on our international relations with our sister Independent African States.

Today I have come to address you on certain matters affecting the security and safety of our Nation, and the progress and welfare of our people.

As you know, five persons have recently been found guilty by the Courts of the offense of treason. They have taken part in a conspiracy to overthrow by unlawful means the established Constitution of the country. After hearing the full evidence in Court, a jury of twelve Ghanaian citizens returned against them a unanimous verdict of "guilty."

In consequence, a sentence of death was passed on them.

Prior to this, a sentence of death had been passed on five other persons by a Special Court presided over by three judges of the Supreme Court. In accordance with these verdicts, the following ten persons, namely: Teiko Tagoe, Anum Yemoh, Joseph Adotei Addo, Malam Mama Tula, Joseph Quaye Mensah, Robert Benjamin Otchere, Joseph Yaw Manu, Tawiah Adamafio, Ako Adjei, H. H. Cofie Crabbe, are due to be hanged.

I need not remind the House of the series of criminal attempts and conspiracies which have been made against my life and against the security of the State since 1953. It is sufficient only to mention:

(a) The Bomb incident at my residence in Accra New Town in 1953,

99

(b) The Alavanyo Training Camp incident in 1957.

(c) The secret attempt made in 1958 by certain Ghanaians to purchase one thousand tons of hand grenades through an European, Dr. Opparvar.

(d) The "T" Junction Plot involving ex-Captain Awhaity, R. R. Amponsah, M. K. Apaloo and others in 1958.

(e) The Gbedemah Conspiracy and the 1961 strike in the Sekondi-Takoradi area.

(f) The 1962 Kukulungu bomb incident, followed by a series of bomb outrages in Accra.

(f) The 1964 Flagstaff House shooting incident.

Since the eve of our independence the imperialists and neo-colonialists have sought persistently to destroy us and the things for which we stand.

In truth. therefore, there has been one conspiracy. The hand that threw the bomb in 1953 is, historically, the same hand that threw the Kulungu bomb in 1962, and did the shooting at Flagstaff House in 1964 which caused the death of a senior security officer, Salifu Dagarti. It is the same hand behind the forgery of photographs, anonymous letters of threats to kill and destroy and the dissemination of naked lies without even the pretence of evidence.

They have failed to destroy us with their violence. They now resort to a sustained campaign of slander and calumny in a vain attempt to distort our image.

But why is their hue and cry so strident against us now?

Let me bring to light the central meaning of the attacks on me and Ghana. It is not out of any concern for civil liberty that they attack us. When they attack us it is because we threaten their interest in Ghana and Africa. All the rest of their pretensions are a hogwash. What is it of which they complain of Ghana? That we oppose their control over our continent and that we wish to develop our own well-being and not their enrichment.

100

That is our only crime in their eyes. They see that Africa is on the threshold of a new life: they know that the success of the O. A. U. Conference at Accra this year will be a significant turning point in African history. By attacking us the neo-colonialists and imperialists are in fact aiming at the prevention of our unity in Africa.

Many of you may have seen the photograph reproduced recently by the London *Daily Express* purporting to depict the horror and misery suffered by Ghanaians in our prisons. My first comment on being shown this picture was: "What a healthy bunch of men! But who are they?" They did not look like Ghanaians to me and I did not recognise any of them as Kofi this or Kojo that.

When I read the caption and the scurrilous article that went with it, I was amazed. Then I wondered: "Whose side is the *Express* on, anyhow? For whose benefit, in whose interest, do they forge such a photograph? On the one hand they go to great pains to write about the appalling treatment meted out to our detainees, whilst on the other, they produce a photograph of a group of healthy, strapping men, their eyes bright and alert, skin shiny, faces free from lines of care or worry, bodies firm and well fed, free from scares or wounds, lounging calmly and relaxed, taking infinite care, it seems, not to put too much pressure on those flimsy anklets and that fine string of best Woolworth metal chain in case they break them before the photographer has finished his job. In any event, it would have been interesting if the *Daily Express* had named the men in the photograph, if they were not after mischief.

All I can say is that if the men in this picture are hardship cases, a lot of us wouldn't mind changing places with them.

This phoney picture does more than merely disprove, on the face of it, the story the *Daily Express* has tried to put over. It exposes and highlights exactly what we in Ghana know such stories to be, namely the wicked invention, the evil imaginings and demented ravings of those who, in their desperation to salvage the remnants of colonialism, imperialism and neo-colonialism, will stop at nothing to bring discredit on Kwame Nkrumah and Ghana.

Fed by journalists and editors who have sold not only their minds but their spirit and souls, and supported by traitors, reactionaries and cheap sensationalists, this type of gutter press believes that if it can destroy the image of Kwame Nkrumah it will make a valuable contribution towards his downfall. Do they know where they are heading? After Kwame Nkrumah, what then? Let them know that whatever they do, Africa will never be the same for them again.

To those who appear to be so concerned about the conditions in our prisons to the extent of even forging photographs about them, we offer a challenge. The Government of Ghana has decided to invite representatives of the Christian Council, the Archbishop of the Catholic Church of Ghana, Bishop R. R. Roseveare of the Anglican Church of Ghana, Bishop Bowers, the Catholic Bishop of Accra, representatives of the Muslim Council and the Red Cross of Ghana to inspect the conditions in our prisons and let the world know the truth.

After experiencing these attempts by the neo-colonialist press to distort the truth of what is happening in Ghana, it is interesting to note the impressions of someone who recently visited this country to see Ghana for himself. In the *London Times* of 25th February, 1965, Mr. James Johnson, a British Member of Parliament, on his return from Ghana is reported to have said that Ghana "was buzzing like a hive with new development schemes."

There is lot of loose talk about Ghana in the press, but he believed that Ghana was an example to Africa in economic development. "Whatever people outside Africa might say about President Nkrumah, he has done a great deal for his people. "If I was a Ghanaian," he said, "I would support him."

The treason trial have been clear to all who can see, to all who are not inspired by malice towards us, to all who can understand, what pressures are brought to bear upon a militant State fighting for independence and well-being of Africa. Plots against Ghana and against my life were put into action. They have been foiled. Those who have so dishonoured themselves are in custody.

Many think that these criminals should be obliged to pay the full penalty for treason. Public feeling in Ghana is aroused and united in its condemnation of those who would have destroyed our achievements to serve their ambition and the evil purposes of those who use them. I understand the feeling of my people and I am moved by their support for me and their indignation against the traitors of Ghana.

Ghana is a confident nation. We know the plots against us. We know who master-minds them and who is used on behalf of conspiracy.

Our answer to those who conspire to destroy us, who attack us when we find their perfidy and who condemn us when we arraign their agents and stooges, is to demonstrate our confidence in ourselves and the unity and solidarity of our people.

Ours is a nation dedicated to the emancipation of man from exploitation and cruelty and unending cycle of oppression. The imperialists and neo-colonialists, sick in mind and vicious in their behaviour, might well emulate the magnanimity of their would-be victims. To them I say: Physician heal thyself!

I repeat again our offer to present our further evidence against Busia, Gbedemah, Kwow Richardson, Taylor and their evil and criminal associates, evidence which is conclusive against these traitors who spread lies about Ghana. Our offer to invite the United Nations to appoint a tribunal to try them faces them and their newspaper supporters with the test they must meet. If they are frightened to come to Accra let the tribunal hear our evidence in a sister African State. This challenge is directed as well to those in the world who malign us. Let them take note of Ghana's stand. Let them come to Ghana and see for themselves. We are a nation on the move.

I know the public feeling in this matter, but, after long nights of serious and careful reflection, I have decided to commute the death sentences passed by the Court on the ten persons convicted of treason against the State, to sentences of twenty years' imprisonment each. It is an expression of our confidence in our people and of our respect for life that we do not stoop to emulate the imperialists, neo-colonialists and their agents, or those agents who serve them. A nation dedicated to the advancement of its people needs no other safeguard than their devotion, their militancy and willingness to defend their achievements, their President and their country.

As you know, in consequence of the series of subversive activities and bomb outrages in the country to which I have referred already, a number of persons are under preventive detention. These people sought to serve our enemies. Here again after serious consideration, I have caused a review of these cases to be made and I shall grant an amnesty to those in detention whose release will not directly endanger the security of the State.

Let no one mistake our clemency for weakness. On the contrary, it should be taken as a warning and assurance that our security forces will be even more vigilant and ever ready to deal swiftly and effectively with any anti-State activities. Let those who continue to plot inside and outside this country against our people, whether they call themselves the "United Party in Exile" or the "Atomic Wing of the Party," be warned that we shall no longer tolerate their diabolical and senseless activities, which in the past have cost this nation many precious lives.

In some countries in Africa persons accused of plotting against the State have been summarily dealt with and executed. The neo-colonialists are mute about this. But this should not be an example for us to follow, because whatever we do in Ghana is of no significance beyond our boundaries. The performance of Ghana is viewed as a yardstick with which to measure everything African.

All our efforts and inspirations at home must be geared to one purpose and one grand objective. We believe that by one mighty continental effort, the African States can generate a united force that can brave an imperialist storm, and break its way through the obstacles of neo-colonialist obstruction. In this task all of us, parliamentarians, politicians, academicians, journalists, workers, farmers all sections of our population have a part to play.

We have the blessing of the wealth of our vast resources, the power of our talent and the potentialities of our people. Let us grasp now the opportunities before us and meet the challenge to our survival.

Mr. Speaker, as I have always emphasised, Africa cannot co-exist with imperialism. We cannot co-exist with colonialism or neo-colonialism. There can never be co-existence between poverty and

104

plenty, between developing countries and the forces that militate against their progress and development. We must be prepared at all times to fight and conquer these anachronisms of the twentieth century and rid our Continent of them.

We look forward to the early establishment of a Continental Union Government of Africa which will throw the whole weight and might of a united Africa to the support of world peace and prosperity.

There is a battle to be fought, there are obstacles to be overcome. There is a world struggle for human dignity to be won. Let us address ourselves seriously to the supreme tasks that lie ahead. To accomplish these aims, Africa must unite.

I leave you to your deliberations and may you be guided by Providence in the supreme interest of the nation.

17

THE ATTEMPTED ASSASSINATION OF PRESIDENT HAMANI DIORI

ALLEGATIONS CONCERNING THE ATTEMPTED ASSASSINATION OF THE PRESIDENT OF THE REPUBLIC OF NIGER

April 1965

The attention of the Government of Ghana has been drawn to newspaper and radio reports designed to associate the name of Ghana with the recent attempt to assassinate President Hamani Diori of Niger.

As the picture of the Nouackhott deliberations unfolds, one can see the full force of the plot that was hatched there against Ghana. For any one to suggest that while Ghana is fully occupied with preparations for receiving the O.A.U. Heads of State in its capital this year, it will at the same time prepare plots to assassinate or remove the very Heads of State who are to be the Guests of our Government in Accra, is to exceed the limit of reason and good sense. Ghana may be passionate to a fault about the need for African Unity based on a Union Government, that is, one Government for all Africa, but the Government of Ghana cannot pursue that goal so zealously as to seek to destroy the very leaders who are to compose that Government, even before they have had a chance to discuss the practical ways and means of achieving it.

If every plot hatched against a Head of State in Africa were instigated and supported by a sister Head of State and its Government, then the President of Ghana who has miraculously survived more than four such attempts on his life within the last three years would have the foremost right to complain of subversion from sister states where there are known to be Ghanaian refugees who are active in their plotting against him and his life.

While we express shock and horror at the attempt on the life of the President of the Niger Republic, no one can deceive the world that some of those who met in Nouackhott wish to use every pretext they can seize upon to justify their declared intention to boycott the Accra O.A.U. Summit Conference. If this were not so, how would any one wish to tell the world that a man from the Niger imprisoned by the Niger Government for over a year and released only in October last year and who is reported to have told his interrogators that he acquired his hand grenades from a state adjacent to his own could have planned his plot from Ghana and from nowhere else?

Do we need further evidence of the wicked machinations of the imperialists and neo-colonialists to create dissension among the African States, thereby destroying the early establishment of a Continental Union Government which they so dread?

The Government of Ghana wants to make it plain to friends and foes that the fantastic allegations being made against Ghana are fictitious, fabricated and completely false.

The Government of Ghana considers that the alleged evidence linking the assassination attempt with Ghanaian sources, is part of the fabricated propaganda and lies now being circulated throughout the world against Ghana mainly because of the desire of the imperialists and neo-colonialists and their agents and cohorts to undermine the success of the forthcoming O.A.U. Conference in Accra.

OSAGYEFO'S LETTER TO HAMANI DIORI

My dear President and Brother,

I write to confirm my telegram congratulating you on your escape from the recent attempt on your life. In doing so I wish to express my shock and horror at the statement supposed to have been made by you that I personally had anything to do with this incident.

If this report is confirmed, then all I can say is that the enemies of the O.A.U., the enemies of the Union Government of Africa, and the enemies of Africa itself, must be behind such a fabrication with the sole purpose of sowing dissension and discord among us. They are doing this in the obvious belief that in this way they can undermine the success of the O.A.U. meeting in Accra.

107

Of all the African Heads of State you are the one to be fully aware of the personal and strenuous efforts that I have been making in my desire to resolve the misunderstanding between Niger and Ghana and to bring all the Independent African States together.

I would therefore like to take this opportunity to urge upon you to get this monstrous fabrication out of your mind. As the Koran points out, a man whose heart is pure fears nothing, for Allah is with him.

With my brotherly greetings,

Yours very sincerely,
KWAME NKRUMAH

18

OUR ECONOMIC SITUATION

EASTER MESSAGE TO THE NATION

April 17, 1965

GOOD EVENING, FRIENDS AND COMRADES,

Easter is usually a time for meditation and reflection. I speak to you this evening in order to bring to your notice something that requires the serious reflection of us all.

It is common knowledge that this nation of ours, our Ghana, is numbered among the leading nations of Africa. We are regarded as part of the vanguard in the struggle against all forms of imperialism on the African continent. We are numbered among those emergent nations that believe in making progress by relying principally on ourselves and on our own resources. We are in the forefront of the vanguard of the African Revolution.

Ours is a hard struggle calling for sustained effort and sacrifice, for constant vigilance, for unrelenting struggle against the forces of imperialism, colonialism and neo-colonialism. But we are making progress along this road. Our efforts are bearing fruit. Every Ghanaian can testify to this. Our enemies and detractors admit it. Their persistence in misrepresenting our endeavours, their fury in denouncing us, their veiled and open threats of blackmail—all stem from an admission that Ghana is forging ahead, and her example may become a light for other emergent African nations.

Our infrastructure of power, transport and communications is far ahead of what is available in most other countries. Our economy is rapidly expanding. Our educational system is one of the most comprehensive and liberal in the world. Our standard of living is very high and compares favourably with most countries of the world. The current issue of *Venture* published by the Fabian Society, the intellectual wing of the British Labour Party has this to say about Ghana:—

"The problems of Ghana are typical of Africa—typical but not average. The wealth of the country, the avoidance of the aping of Europe . . . the explicit recognition of needs and possibilities; these make Ghana the test case of Africa—if she succeeds there is hope for all, if she fails who else can succeed?"

But we have our problems. Which country, may I ask, is entirely free of problems? Indeed we can number ourselves among the more fortunate countries of the world. Our problems are those of growth. They are not the problems of stagnation or of decay. Some of our new factories are not producing as efficiently as they should. But efficiency in production has become a problem only because we have made progress in setting up the factories. We experience serious problems with the distribution of consumer goods. But this has become a problem only because we have made progress in wresting the control of our domestic trade from the foreign firms which formerly dominated this vital field of our national economy. The point I wish to emphasise, and which we all as Ghanaians must take seriously to heart, is that our current economic problems have arisen because we are moving forward. As we solve these problems so we shall move into the realms of economic independence for our nation and personal prosperity for ourselves as individuals.

We Ghanaians are not in the habit of shying away from our difficulties, or shirking our responsibilities. We are a confident people. We face our problems squarely. And we are determined to surmount these difficulties.

The greatest single problem facing us today as a nation is that of economic administration. Our factories must be run more efficiently. Imported consumer goods must be better distributed. Essential consumer goods at reasonable prices must be made available to all, and I mean every single person in Ghana.

Our continued progress in the economic field demands that we attain these objectives. The best interests of our people demand that we find speedy and effective remedies for these short-comings.

It is important for you to be fully informed on the basic facts of our economic situation. It is our Government's deliberate policy to cut down on our imports of consumer goods. Such action will enable us to save on our foreign exchange and spend more on imports of machines, equipments, spare parts and raw materials for our factories. This much you know. What is more, you know that this is a wise and necessary step in support of the declared policy of our industrialisation and the modernisation of our agriculture.

But the practical implementation of this policy is not generally understood. In practice, we have cut down on our imports of consumer goods in such a way as to reduce drastically the non-essentials and luxuries. We have, on the other hand, continued to bring in the essential consumer goods in the quantities imported last year. Indeed, we have, in some cases, even increased our imports of these essentials above the 1964 level. It is therefore not accurate to attribute the current shortages of some of these goods to a cut in the allocation of foreign exchange for the purchase of these goods. I want, however, to assure you and the Nation that the Government will continue to make available all the foreign exchange needed to cover the import of these essential consumer goods until such a time as our own factories could produce them in the required quantities for our home consumption.

But the cause of the current shortages must be traced to some other source. The source of our current trade difficulties is our machinery for economic administration. The State agencies connected with the importation and distribution of these goods have not functioned as efficiently as desired. Their distribution network does not cover the country effectively. Their methods of operation are slow and too much hidebound by bureaucratic routine and red tape. The goods that should go directly to the consumers are diverted either through the passbook system to other firms or to an army of profiteering middlemen made up of public men, their wives and their relations. The passbook has become the instrument for diverting goods that should have been ordered directly to the people, at reasonable prices, into the hands of wives and relations of unscrupulous people. In this regard, Ministers, Regional and District Commissioners, Civil and Public Servants, Party Officials, Parliamentarians, Managing Directors and Managers of Corporations, Factories and State Farms, should and must set the highest and finest example worthy of socialist emulation. Those who hoard and sell consumer goods at exorbitant prices to the public, thus enriching themselves

111

and their relations at the expense and to the inconvenience of the very people they are called upon to serve are not worthy of the Nation's cause. Imagine a packet of sugar costing, say, one shilling and two pence. By the time it passes through the hands of three or four racketeers and hoarders, and reaches the consumer the price has increased three or four times. We cannot tolerate this state of affairs in Ghana. The price inspectors have not always been helpful to the public. Either because of their individual weaknesses or their connection with men in high positions and State functionaries, these price inspectors still have not succeeded in checking the hoarding of goods or their sale above the control price. In many cases, they are in league with the profiteers.

These failings are very serious. We take them seriously. I would like to remind those public men who lack the conscience of doing their duty to the public that other countries have passed through a phase similar to what we are today going through. Some countries have resorted to large scale dismissals; others have found it necessary to imprison; and others even went so far as to shoot such shameless elements.

Comrades and Countrymen,

What are we doing to cope with these problems?

We have organised and streamlined the Ministry of Agriculture. And you know of our decision to reorganise the Ministry of Trade. There is now to be a Ministry of Foreign Trade which will handle a imports of the essential consumer goods from all parts of the world. The Ministry will operate for some time under my direction. 1 addition, there will be a Ministry of Internal, that is, home Trad This Ministry will concentrate on the efficient distribution within th country of all imported consumer goods as well as produc produced by our factories and state farms. It is our belief that th division of effort will result in increased efficiency and benefit to tl consumer.

I have ordered an inquiry into the system of passbooks and t so-called "chits." In addition, it is my intention that all racketeerir profiteering and illegal dealings in the retail and wholesale trade consumer goods, and the inefficient working of our price control machinery should be thoroughly examined and brought to light and dealt with.

I have directed that the work of this inquiry be done expeditiously. And as soon as the findings are available, I shall see to it that the necessary administrative changes and controls take immediate effect. We are determined that these essential goods will get to the people in the needed amounts at the right times and at the right prices.

You will remember that four years ago, in my Dawn Broadcast, I called upon the leading members in the Party and in the State machinery to draw a line between politics and business. I must today repeat this warning. One of the causes of our present difficulties is the misuse of high Party and State positions. Some of us who hold these positions of trust have allowed ourselves to be lured into business speculation and profit seeking. We use the influence that our position gives us to coerce or induce persons connected with our trade machinery and with our price control into handing over lucrative but nefarious trade to our relations, wives and friends. This state of affairs must stop and stop forthwith.

I am resolved on my part that, in this matter of trade in essential consumer goods, the interest of the general public must be upheld at all times. But your Government need the support and the co-operation of every honest citizen and dedicated Party activist. You can help by immediately reporting any case of hoarding or selling at above the control price to the Ministry of Internal Trade where with the assistance of the Attorney-General's Office a special machinery has been set up to deal with this.

Let us all resolve to wage a relentless war against all those engaged in the dirty game of extorting wealth from the workers and the masses. We must smoke out these hoarders and profiteers from the holes of their illegal warehouses.

Let us step up the fight against bribery, corruption, avarice and nepotism, the vices that seem to sap the faith in our Revolution and Socialist construction.

Let us resist and check those who by loose talk and propaganda try to undermine the sound principles upon which our foreign trade is based.

COUNTRYMEN, the Party and the Government will continue to be guided by the present and future needs of the Nation and the highest interests of the people in general.

Let us therefore rededicate ourselves to the service of the Nation and work towards the achievement of the goals and ideals we set before our people and the Nation.

I wish you all a happy Easter.

Good night.

19

TRUE FREEDOM FOR ALL

FOURTH AFRO-ASIA SOLIDARITY CONFERENCE

Winneba
May 10, 1965

DELEGATES OF THE AFRO-ASIAN SOLIDARITY CONFERENCE,
DISTINGUISHED GUESTS,

At this Conference of solidarity between the peoples of Africa and Asia, even more than in the preceding ones, grave and momentous decisions will have to be taken to meet new emergencies in the conflict between imperialism and the majority of mankind.

It cannot be otherwise: Afro-Asian solidarity itself emerged from this conflict. It emerged from our common determination to destroy the remnants of colonialism, and our common need to repulse the assaults of neo-colonialism in its efforts to recover the ground lost by imperialism in the great socialist revolutions and world wide struggles for national liberation which followed the Second World War.

Each new wave of national liberation and decolonization has swept imperialism into ever-deepening economic and political crises. Its desperate measures to save itself from extinction have made all efforts at peaceful co-existence and a peaceful transition to a world freed from national, racial and economic oppression, harder and harder to attain.

We still hope for an end to the Cold War. We still hope that enslaved peoples, like those of South Africa, Southern Rhodesia and the Portuguese colonies, will liberate themselves without an armed struggle. We still hope that neo-colonialism's incessant search for military bases, puppet governments and regimes, hidden allies and disguised instruments of exploitation will be abandoned. We still hope that the economic warfare which the industrialised Western nations wage against the developing world will end.

But we meet here as realists who must see things as they are, and not as we would like them to be.

We meet at a time when bombs are falling on the people of Vietnam; when the bullets and bayonets of foreign mercenaries are being used to tyrannise the people of the Congo; when foreign marines and paratroopers have been interposed between the people of the Dominican Republic and their freedom.

We meet at a time when the United Nations has fallen into disarray, and seems incapable of fulfilling its supreme purpose, namely, the maintenance of peace in the world; when the conferences for nuclear disarmament have reached a stalemate which leaves mankind without hope.

We, from the colonial and ex-colonial countries of Africa and Asia, do not need to be told that the military and political convulsions and deadlocks which threaten the peace of mankind do not arise from the malignant influence of the stars, but from the determination of imperialism not to surrender its hold on those areas and peoples which it still holds in captivity, and on those which have gained their independence, but have not yet acquired the economic strength to make that independence a reality.

Not only the bombs, mercenaries and contingents of marines, but also the defiance and obduracy of some industrialised nations at the Economic Conference of the United Nations at Geneva last year, must be considered in your deliberations upon the present world crisis.

Decolonization, national liberation, the Charter of the United Nations, the principles of co-existence and even the possible outbreak of a nuclear conflict—none of these momentous developments in the modern world have caused imperialism to deviate from its course of economic exploitation, or to desist from undermining the independence of nations to make this exploitation possible.

Wherever and whenever we seek the causes of war, we find the answer in economic exploitation, the heart of imperialism. We seek the causes of national and racial oppression, and we find the answer

116

in economic exploitation, the heart of imperialism. We seek the causes of continued undermining of emergent nations, and we find the answer in economic exploitation, the heart of imperialism. If, then, in welcoming you here today, I spend some time dwelling on the economic problems of the Afro-Asian nations, you will readily understand that I am not merely concerned with our economic development but also with world peace and with universal freedom.

In this conference of peoples of the Afro-Asian world, we are not only concerned with peoples who are seeking to defend their independence and to use their independence for social and economic development. We are also concerned with peoples still under the colonial yoke, still enslaved by foreign invaders.

We are not unmindful that for the peoples of South Africa, Mozambique, Angola, Zimbabwe, the so-called Portuguese Guinea, and others, the problems of independence and of neo-colonialism, of economic development and equitable trade, do not arise in the same sharp form as for the independent peoples in this conference. To them we say: Brothers, we know your needs and will not forget them. You are entitled to your freedom at any cost, and if you are only able to gain your freedom by an armed struggle, we will not only consider your wars against the foreign oppressor as just and holy, but we will be prepared to help you as if these were our own wars for our own liberation.

If we say less, and do less at this conference, we shall be making a mockery of the solidarity in whose cause we are here gathered. We shall be doing violence to all the instincts and moral principles which drove us, in the struggles for our own freedom. What is more, we shall be frustrating our own efforts to drive imperialism and neo-colonialism out of our own borders.

It is well known by now that it was this overriding need to free the enslaved part of the African continent and to help our brothers to liberate themselves, which gave the independent nations of Africa the inspiration to achieve the first step towards unity at the Summit Conference in Addis Ababa. It also cannot be unknown to you that I did not believe then, and do not believe now, that anything less than the unity which finds its expression in a Continental Govern-

117

ment of a United Africa, will be an effective force to help in the liberation of the enslaved part of Africa.

It is also true that I do not believe that any of the fundamental problems of the independent states of Africa can be finally solved until a continental government of Africa comes into being. Africa can become a much more effective force in the struggle against imperialism when a continental government has been achieved.

I do not believe that the economic development of Africa can reach an effective stage until Africa's human and material resources have been mobilised under a continental Union Government of Africa. But I do believe (and nothing that has happened or can happen, will swerve me from my belief), that the emergence of a Continental Government of Africa will immediately make the independent states of Africa a mighty world influence. We shall then be in a far better position to liberate our brothers in colonial bondage and rule, to drive out imperialism and neo-colonialism from our continent, to make us a powerful ally of the Asian peoples in their own struggles against imperialism, and to make us an effective force for world peace.

Whilst, for the peoples struggling against colonialism, the problems and principles of solidarity are comparatively simple, we must remember that there are complicating factors which we must face at this conference. We cannot but deplore divisions which spring up in the ranks of the freedom-fighters of the occupied parts of Africa and Asia. In the face of slavery and domination, how can any divisions be allowed to cause dissensions which will prolong that slavery and domination? If unity is essential for independent peoples in their struggle against imperialism, how much more must it be so for these peoples fighting to throw out a foreign invader and to throw off the chains of slavery?

Solidarity itself raises many problems. Not the least is the presence of political refugees in our independent States. This often causes misunderstandings and hard feelings which militate against our solidarity in the face of the common enemy, imperialism. But the principle of giving refuge to political opponents of a ruling regime are clear and hallowed by custom and international law through the centuries. I have explained my stand fully on at least two occasions, and this is a fitting occasion for me to do so again. Every state has a right, even a duty, to give shelter to political refugees, provided a further duty is observed that this refuge shall not be used for activities against another State. We have observed both the duty of giving shelter and of preventing the abuse of that shelter. All the malicious accusations made against us in this respect are all fabrications employed to undermine our struggle against imperialism and neo-colonialism, and to thwart our efforts to establish a continental Union Government for all Africa.

Distinguished Delegates:

I would like to touch on a further problem which affects you as an organisation of the solidarity of peoples, rather than of governments. It seems to me that provision should be made in your constitution for the admission of more than one political party or movement from each territory represented, provided that such parties or movements are by their programmes and activities, anti-imperialist, anti-colonialist, anti-neo-colonialist and anti-racialist. Beyond that, it seems to me, no good purpose can be served by elaborate inquisitions into the internal affairs of the freedom fighters in colonial countries, and of the political movements in independent countries. It cannot be in the interest of the solidarity of the peoples that any one party or movement should have a vested right to membership of your organisation merely because it was first in the field. In many countries, popular parties and movements ebb and flow.

Delegates:

We meet as a Conference of Afro-Asian Solidarity. Let no one mistake this as a racial alignment. We are neither racists nor racialists although we happen to be non-white in overwhelming numbers on these two continents, and although imperialism today operates from countries where the peoples are predominantly white. We are not here because we come from Africa and Asia, but because we belong to that part of the human race whose lands have been colonised and whose freedom was taken away by the imperialists. We do not forget that the peoples of Latin America, who suffer the same fate as we on the continents of Africa and Asia, are of European as well as of Indian and African origin. These peoples of Latin America and the Carribean have not been deliberately excluded from our solidarity. Our Organisation of Afro-Asian Solidarity developed under circumstances which made the inclusion of the Latin American and the Carribean peoples difficult. But these difficulties must be overcome, and our solidarity with them must be cemented as rapidly as possible. No other peoples have suffered as much from neo-colonialism as the peoples of Latin America and the Carribean. Their solidarity with the peoples of Africa and Asia is as necessary for them as for us, if we are to achieve a final victory over world imperialism.

But Latin America apart, I must emphasize with all the seriousness at my command that we are here to wage a war against a system and not against a race. We are here because we are resolved that any system or regime which owes its existence to the exploitation of man by man, the humiliation of man by man, and the degradation of man by man, cannot and must not be permitted to continue its existence in the world. We are a part of the human race that is determined to free itself from the ravages of colonialism, from the machinations of neo-colonialism, and from the menace of imperialism, irrespective of their racial, national or geographical origins.

We know that we have the support of the mass of progressive opinion outside Africa and Asia. The non-aligned states have shown by their successful deliberations in Belgrade and Cairo that we have allies in Europe and on the American Continent. We should therefore consolidate and reinforce our solidarity with the non-aligned states so that progressive people and organisations throughout the world irrespective of race, colour or creed are mobilised to fight for peace, prosperity and progress.

We are not here for racial prestige. We are here, first of all, to ensure freedom for all who live under colonial bondage or racial oppression. We are here to ensure that the freedom which we have won, and which we will help our brothers to win, will have a true meaning, and not be merely a political facade.

For the peoples represented here who have won their freedom, the main struggle to be waged now is economic, always remembering that every economic struggle is carried on, not in a vacuum, but in a political and social context.

Our independence means much more than merely being free to fly our own flag and to play our own national anthem. It becomes a reality only in a revolutionary framework when we create and sustain a level of economic development capable of ensuring a higher standard of living, proper education, good health and cultural development to all our citizens. If the people are not clothed better, fed better, sheltered better; if the people are not ensured employment, personal dignity and cultural and spiritual advancement, what have they gained by independence? What meaning can independence have for the people, if we throw off political bondage only, and remain in economic and mental subservience?

When we wage battle against imperialism, we in fact wage a political battle directed to an economic end. The imperialists are not cruel or deceitful or destructible because they were born wicked. They are cruel, deceitful war-mongers because they find this the most effective means of economic exploitation. For the imperialist, human values count for nothing and are always subordinated to his quest for profit. When there is profit to be made from being cruel, the imperialist is a devil in human form.

Our economic struggle against imperialism cannot be carried on without coming to grips with the forces of exploitation both at home and abroad. It cannot be waged unless the people themselves are mobilized for the struggle and have a direct interest in the struggle. Nor can it be carried on effectively without full political solidarity and economic co-operation between all the developing countries,

The emergence of African and Asian independence made necessary for imperialism to invent and put into operation methods of exploitation which were almost unknown in the era of colonialism. In the newly-independent countries, indigenous forces had to found as secret partners and agents in the process of exploitation. In trade with the new states, monopolistic and restrictive device had to be found to bring down the prices of crops and material from the developing countries, to raise the cost of their imports, limit their credits, devalue their currencies, undermine their confidence and teach them to live on doles and handouts.

The methods are involved and devious, the aims simple and transparent. The aim of imperialism is to inhibit or slow down the economic development of the ex-colonies, so that they will remain colonies in everything but name.

We call this latest phase of imperialism, neo-colonialism. Our solidarity here will mean very little unless we understand neo-colonialism thoroughly, and plan to wage a struggle against it with the same spirit, courage and determination with which we fought for our political independence.

It is useless thinking that solidarity on any other basis than a struggle against neo-colonialism will rid our continents of imperialism. But the struggle against neo-colonialism means putting our own house in order before we can become loyal and effective allies in our common struggle against imperialism.

If a state in Africa or Asia is in the grip of neo-colonialism; if it allows the imperialists to retain their military bases and financial institutions; if it retains the agents of imperialism in its administration and armed forces; if it encourages its citizens to enter into partnerships with imperialist companies and corporations—how can that state wage a struggle against neo-colonialism, the new phase of imperialism?

The mass of the people can never become the agents or partners of neo-colonialism. The function of neo-colonialism is to exploit, not to share with the people. In like manner, imperialism, the father of neo-colonialism, does not share; it grabs and exploits the people. It is the people, therefore, and only the people, who can save an African or Asian state from neo-colonialism and imperialism.

Here, there is need to draw a line between foreign investments that grab and exploit, and those investments which help in the development of an emergent and developing nation. Foreign investments that co-operate with the development of an emergent nation, and without strings attached, must be seen as of a quite different nature from the known pattern of imperialist exploitation, even if in the process they earn normal returns.

Where and when the people are in control of their state, the waves of imperialism and neo-colonialism must recede. Where control of the state is not vested in the people, imperialism takes over, with the same effect for the people as in the days of colonial rule.

Is it surprising, therefore, that the struggle against imperialism and neo-colonialism takes its sharpest form as a peoples' revolutionary struggle against puppet governments and regimes?

The Dominican Republic is not very large in size or population, but its name may still become symbolic of a new stage in open and indisguised aggression by imperialism against a national liberation movement. There, the intervention to suppress a popular uprising has followed closely on pronouncements that wars of national liberation will not be tolerated.

It is difficult to believe that this conference will not reject the contention of the imperialists that they are entitled to decide what form a struggle of national liberation must take. If we were to accept their contention, we, the people of Africa and Asia, and the freedom fighters of South Africa, Angola, Mozambique, Portuguese Guinea and Zimbabwe, would have to abandon great parts of our continent and many millions of our people to perpetual slavery. This we will never do. And even if we become so lost to honour and humanity as to do so, the peoples of these countries would ignore us and in spite of us continue their struggle for national liberation alone.

The shadow of the struggle in South-East Asia must fall very deeply on a Conference of Afro-Asian solidarity. I know that this conference will spend many hours discussing the best means of using Afro-Asian solidarity to compel the imperialist aggressors to withdraw, so that the people of Vietnam can decide their own destiny.

The conflict in Vietnam, which daily threatens to escalate into wider war, has a political origin and can only be resolved by the Vietnamese people themselves; therefore, hands off Vietnam! Any attempt to impose a military solution will be short-sighted and futile. Recently various approaches have been made to create a favourable atmosphere for negotiations to resolve the conflict in Vietnam. These approaches have not been successful because one essential ingredient has been missing. For any appeal for negotiations to merit consideration, it must be preceded by the withdrawal of foreign military presence. With the best will in the world, one finds it extremely difficult to understand the view held in some quarters that air strikes on North Vietnam are calculated to put the North Vietnam Government into a suitable frame of mind to enter into negotiations. The bombing has not led to such a result so far, and it is unlikely to do so. What it is doing is to increase the risk of widening the conflict into a catastrophic war.

A situation in South-East Asia which has become a source of great embarrassment to all Afro-Asians and a threat to Afro-Asian solidarity, is the distressing conflict between Indonesia and Malaysia. I have on many occasions appealed for negotiated settlement. I have also on many occasions offered my good offices to assist in seeking settlements. I am convinced that all of us gathered here would earnestly like to see a speedy and peaceful settlement to these conflicts from which none of the parties could benefit. But the condition prior to a successful negotiation is the withdrawal of imperialist presence in this area. Of even greater seriousness, neither Indonesia nor Malaysia could afford to divert resources sorely needed for development into a conflict so easily avoidable. I would therefore like to appeal once again to my friends, President Sukarno of Indonesia and Prime Minister Tunku Abdul Rahman of Malaysia, to start talking around the conference table and bring these conflicts to an end without delay.

The conflict between India and Pakistan is of a different nature. It is a border dispute between two emergent and developing countries. Even though I have on many occasions appealed for a negotiated settlement, and on many occasions offered my good services, I would like to appeal to Prime Minister Shastri of India and President Ayub Khan of Pakistan to make another effort at a peaceful settlement between their two sister States. The point here to be borne in mind is that there is a fundamental difference between territorial dispute involving two emergent nations, and territorial dispute involving an emergent nation and imperialism, and a territorial dispute between two emergent nations teleguided by imperialism.

There is no doubt that the imperialist counter-attack against human freedom and progress is mounting in ferocity and volume throughout the world. The imperialists are behind all the conflicts among the emergent and developing nations. They are set on a course which must spell disaster for themselves, but which can also work great havoc for humanity. Our solidarity therefore has become more important than ever before. It must be widened and strengthened by establishing close links with the peoples of Latin America and the Carribean. It must gather new and greater strength by establishing close links amongst ourselves in our struggle against open imperialism and neo-colonialism.

A united Africa in solidarity with the peoples of Asia and Latin America, will constitute an invincible force which imperialism can neither subvert nor conquer.

The anti-imperialist world now embraces such an overwhelming majority of mankind that the imperialists will only continue with their campaigns of military and economic aggression and propaganda, if they are convinced that they can destroy the unity of the developing nations of Africa and Asia.

As we meet here today, with large portions of the African continent still enslaved, with South-East Asia in flames, with our economies under attack, with the majority of our peoples still in want, with nuclear armaments piling up, and with mounting imperialist aggression recklessly escalating conflicts which may lead to a nuclear world war, we are bound to ask ourselves: Who has the right today to jeopardise the unity of the anti-imperialist world ?

Who stands to gain by dissensions amongst us? Who can withstand us, if we can make our solidarity a reality?

Our main preoccupation at this Conference should be to strengthen our solidarity. It seems to me that the main task is to find answers to the problems of organizing our solidarity, of mobilizing our peoples and of giving impetus to the peoples' will to peace and social change.

Just as disunity in our ranks retards the struggle against imperialism, so the agents of neo-colonialism who ride on our backs to influence and power, giving false homage to our solidarity, must be regarded as retarding the struggle against imperialism. There is one test, and one test only for our solidarity: Do we mobilize and rely on the people in the struggle against imperialism in all its forms, or do we relegate the role of the mass of the people to a secondary place in this struggle? I say that only the mass of the people can ensure victory in our struggle.

As you know, the people of Ghana are preparing to act as hosts to the next summit conference of the Organisation of African Unity. We have great hopes that the fruits of your deliberations and the messages of solidarity from this conference will pave the way for the deliberations and accomplishments of the African Summit Conference.

In the name of the people of Ghana, I greet you and welcome you to Ghana. I think I can speak in the name of humanity to beseech you to set aside everything that is not relevant to the task of organizing and consolidating our peoples' solidarity. There was never greater need to exert ourselves to save the world from war and want, and to move forward to find final solutions for the total liberation and sustained progress of mankind.

I wish you successful deliberations.

20

GHANA TELEVISION SERVICE

CEREMONY OF INAUGURATION

July 13, 1965

I am happy to be here with you today, to inaugurate Ghana's Television Service and to share with you and the people of Ghana, the sense of joy and expectancy on this important occasion. We are also here to inaugurate today the expansion of our Sound Broadcasting Service.

The idea of building a Television Service for the education and edification, the enjoyment and entertainment of our people was conceived almost six years ago. At that time, the sceptics declared that the establishment of a truly indigenous Television Service, organised and staffed by Ghanaians was an impossible task. Undaunted, we set up a Television Commission consisting of two experienced officers lent by the Canadian Broadcasting Corporation to make recommendations on the establishment of television in Ghana. The report of this Commission was published in December, 1959, and accepted by the Government. Planning for Ghana television began in earnest, and during the last five years we, and I mean all of you who in one way or the other have contributed to what we see around us today, have worked patiently, diligently and with commendable zeal to build this project.

And may I say here how grateful we are to the overseas personnel who have assisted us in this trying and engaging venture. Some of them are still with us now, and others are no longer with us.

And here, I would like to thank the Canadian Government, who have been so generous to us in their assistance, in equipment and personnel, in connection with the establishment of Ghana's Television. We owe them a great debt of gratitude.

I accept the fine presentation which has just been made to me on behalf of the Marconi Company. The Company has assisted us in no small measure in the construction of our Television transmitters and studio complex. We are grateful to them.

It is the aim of the Government to ensure that all our people have access to Ghana Television. As a result of an agreement between the Government and the Sanyo Company and two other companies in Japan, we have established here the Ghana Sanyo Corporation for the production of television sets in Ghana. The Corporation is at present engaged in building a factory at Tema. It is expected that the construction of this factory will be completed by the end of this year and be ready to go into production in the New Year.

As I have said, the relay services for sound broadcasting will be greatly expanded by building new relay stations particularly in the rural areas. In addition, the Government has established the State Electronic Products Corporation which will produce more relay boxes, transistor sets and other electronic products for the country.

I want to say a special word of appreciation at this time, to the devoted and dedicated work which has been done behind the scenes, by all the Ghanaians who have taken part in this great enterprise. There is no need for me to underline the part played by the Board of the Ghana Broadcasting Corporation and its Chairman, Mr. Cecil Forde, the Director of Television, Mrs. Shirley Du Bois, and the Deputy Director, Mr. Alex Quarmyne. But my commendation will be incomplete if I fail to mention the Chief Engineer, Mr. Oppong and his staff, the Assistant Chief Engineer, Mr. Dentu; the vivacious Head of Programmes, Miss Genoveva Marais, and her team of able and indefatigable producers: the Head of News, Mr. Shang-Simpson, the Acting Head of Film, Mr. Wilcox Amartey; and the Acting Head of Designs, Mr. Francis Adansi. These keen and devoted officers and those working with them have been the key personnel in this important and trying operation. We are proud of them. May they continue to hold aloft the banner of Ghana Television.

And what can I yet say of the film cameramen, designers, newsmen, technicians and the producers, without whom Ghana's Television would not have become the reality it is today. To them all I say—Well done and *Ayekoo*.

I have had the opportunity recently to learn something of the staff structure and conditions of service of the staff of the Ghana Broadcasting Corporation, and the efforts which had been made to improve these conditions. I have given directions in this matter, and the Board of the Corporation will very shortly announce promotions and changes in the conditions of service, which will go quite a long way to meet the problems which now face some of you.

And now, I want to express a warm welcome to the group of Television Technicians who have come here from the Federal Republic of Germany to assist us in the production of Television programmes. These Technicians who have been sponsored by the Friedrich Ebert Foundation, a private organisation in the Federal Republic of Germany, will work in close co-operation with the staff of Ghana Television, and will concentrate mainly on the production of technical educational television programmes. These will include films on all aspects of science and technical training, agricultural techniques, and a special series of films for the teaching of vocational work and practical lessons for home and school. These programmes will be made available to support the programmes produced by the regular staff of Ghana Television. In this way the quality and content of our Television Service, as a whole, will be improved and enhanced, in the playing of its full part in the life of our society.

We have, deliberately, postponed the opening of Ghana's Television until we could be absolutely sure that we were ready to provide a Service in accord with our national aspirations, and in conformity with our socialist objectives. When I addressed Parliament in October, 1963, I stated then the basic purposes behind Ghana's Television. This is what I said:

"Ghana's Television will be used to supplement our educational programme and foster a lively interest in the world around us. It will not cater for cheap entertainment nor commercialism. Its paramount object will be education in the broadest and purest sense. Television must assist in the socialist transformation of Ghana."

Ghana's Television, which we are inaugurating today, will be judged by the extent to which it fulfills these aims. Our Television

Service should be African in its outlook; and in its content, even though it may express and reflect outside; and foreign experiences, should remain geared to the needs of Ghana and Africa. It must reflect and promote the highest national and social ideals of our ideology and society. In this endeavour, the Board of the Ghana Broadcasting Corporation, together with all the executives and staff of the Television Service are charged with a great and onerous responsibility. It will be their duty to ensure that the professional standards attained by Ghana Television are comparable to the best anywhere in the world. It will also be their duty to think about and develop new techniques, improving and designing new equipment and new ways to achieve a more effective use of our Television medium.

Now, a final word on Television.

We must recognize the prime importance of the creative writer, whose skill and inventiveness are so essential and indispensable to Television. It is the Ghanaian writer who can adequately express the essence of the Party's ideology, the arts, music and drama, and culture of a growing and advancing nation, and the spirit and emotions of our people which must find expression in our Television.

Ghanaian writers must, therefore, be closely associated with the planning, development, and production of all our Television programmes. To this end, our writers and artists must be consulted in all discussions of the content of their scripts, and the use to which the scripts will eventually be put in the preparation of programmes for Television. It is to Ghanaian writers that Ghana must look for our future cultural progress, and Ghana Television should offer them a wonderful opportunity and an effective medium through which they can reach the masses of the people. An idea or a movement achieves reality only when it reaches the masses.

For this same reason, Ghana Television must not be isolated from the life of the people and other aspects of our traditional art and culture. A Television drama or comedy should be a co-operative or co-ordinating effort between the script writer, the film producer, the technical expert, and the Television programme organizer. It is to encourage this co-operative endeavour that we have established a

130

Film Television and Broadcasting Training School here, in which instruction and guidance is provided, under one roof, for script writers as well as for cameramen, designers, newsmen and other film technicians. The best artists in the theatre, film and literature must share their talents with Television, in order that all the Ghanaian arts may reach that communal outburst of creativity, which has marked the great periods of art in other parts of the world.

Ghana is on the threshold of the fulfilment of her long suppressed genius and impulses, and it is only by a co-operative effort that we can bring all the talents of our nation to bear on the struggle for the socialist construction of Ghana. But socialism is an epoch; it cannot be achieved in a day. It is only by sustained effort and determination that it can be realized.

What I have said about Television applies equally well to Sound Broadcasting Service, whose extended programmes and expanded services I have also the great pleasure to inaugurate today. May I at the outset congratulate the Director of Sound Broadcasting, Mr. Coleman, and his staff for their efforts in the arduous task of building the Ghana Broadcasting System.

In order to improve the standards of our national broadcasting services, the Government has recently taken certain decisions which are to be put into effect immediately. First, all the existing three national networks of the Broadcasting Service will be converted into one single network, and all our national transmitters will carry the same programmes throughout the country.

Secondly, the number of hours during which Broadcasting programmes are heard on the radio will be increased and the contents of the programmes will also be considerably augmented and improved. For this purpose, the new Broadcasting transmitters at Ejura will be used to reinforce those in Accra. They will, however, carry the same single network.

Thirdly, the Broadcasting Relay Service will be expanded by building new relay stations particularly in the rural areas and by increasing the coverage of the existing stations.

In support of our national services, the External Service of our

Broadcasting Corporation has been greatly expanded. As a result, the voice of Ghana will from now on be heard all over Africa and far around the world, carrying the message of African aspiration and progress, African emancipation and national unity.

Our Broadcasting Service should struggle ceaselessly to make itself the people's service. It should identify itself fully with the people's aspirations for a fuller life. It should continue to fight uncompromisingly against the forces militating against our progress. It will be its task to expose and unmask imperialism, colonialism and neo-colonialism in all its forms and manifestations, and support our endeavours for the political unification of our Continent. It must blaze the trail of socialism, it must be the *Okyeame* of Ghana's development, and its economic and industrial advancement. It should, above all, strive to enlighten and uplift our people and keep before them the torch of Ghana's advancement.

All who are employed in our Television Service and our Sound Broadcasting Service have a unique opportunity, therefore, to play a vital role in the development of Ghana and in our struggle to eradicate from our society superstition, ignorance and illiteracy, and create in the minds of our people, through television and broadcasting, an awareness of the benefits to Ghana of modern science and technology.

I am confident that you will all bring to this task the highest sense of dedication and devotion. Let us hope that as a result of these new Services, the growth of socialist consciousness among the people will be hastened through our Television and Sound Broadcasting, and that fresh vistas on the world will be opened to them. We also expect that through your programmes, the struggle for the African liberation movement, for freedom and independence, the struggle against imperialism, colonialism and neo-colonialism, and the ever-continuing efforts for the attainment of peace and security throughout the world, will ever be maintained.

I have great pleasure in inaugurating Ghana's Television Service, and the expansion of our National and External Broadcasting Services. I wish those who work here happiness and success.

21

SIGNIFICANT LANDMARK

CLOSING SESSION OF THE
THIRD O.A.U. SUMMIT CONFERENCE

State House
Accra
October 26, 1965

BROTHERS AND COLLEAGUES,

Five days ago, I welcomed you to Accra in the name of the Government and people of Ghana, and opened this Conference, the Second Session of the Assembly of Heads of State and Government. We have come to the end of our deliberations and it now remains for me to express once again the sense of honour that we feel in having been privileged to play host to this Conference at this important time in the history of our continent.

We can say with pride and justification that this has been a successful Conference and that it has carved a significant landmark in our efforts to achieve the purposes set out in the Charter of the O.A.U.

But let us not forget that the masses of, Africa are impatient to see their hopes and aspirations quickly fufilled. They are; looking to the O.A.U. to achieve this in the early establishment of an All-African Union Government.

We have taken important decisions on Southern Rhodesia, on the problem of refugees and subversion and many other matters which will strengthen our Organisation. The decisions we have taken will demonstrate to the world that in spite of the manoeuvres of the imperialist and the neo-colonialists we can take our destiny into our own hands, tackle our problems realistically and find solutions in a spirit of harmony. Our resolution on Southern Rhodesia is a clear demonstration of our solidarity with our brothers in that country, and our determination that their fate shall not be bargained away.

With regard to the problem of refugees I think that our deliberations have confirmed the fact that this is a problem with which we will have to live, and it is a great credit to us all that we have taken a decision on it which unmistakably reveals that our attitude to this problem has the essential humanity of the African people. We have by our decisions on this problem clearly defined the limits within which people seeking asylum can be given sanctuary. It is also important that the problem of subversion should have been clearly defined and an attempt made to contain it and prevent it from bringing dissension between States of the Organisation.

As I indicated in my opening address to this Assembly, unless there is adequate machinery for the implementation of the decisions of the Assembly of the O.A.U., and also of tackling problems which may arise while it is in recess, the Organisation will become a body notorious for its endless paper decisions but with no means of implementing them. Let me illustrate. If our Assembly had not been in session at this time what could we have done about the serious situation in Southern Rhodesia? Could we have in our various capitals agreed on a common course of action? Could we have expressed our resolution to the world as we did three nights ago? I doubt it. Quite apart from emergencies such as Southern Rhodesia, the Executive Council I proposed could be useful in developing long term recommendations for the consideration of the Assembly of Heads of State and Government. This would save considerable time and effort when the Assembly actually convenes. As you know four days is totally inadequate to decide important matters affecting the destiny of Africa. It is clear that if the affairs of our States were conducted in this way there would be no progress or development. Programmes affecting the future of Africa require much more detailed investigation, analysis and consideration, and it would be most useful if an organ were established to do the spade work for our consideration at our regular meetings. I do not wish to dwell on this at length. I think that we are all agreed in principle on the necessity of establishing such a machinery.

Mr. Chairman, it is clear from the careful and lengthy consideration of my proposal to establish an Executive Council of the O.A.U. and from the voting, that at least three-quarters of the members present who took part in the vote on the question of setting up an Executive Council are in favour of my proposal being examined by a special commission. The resolution was not adopted because our Charter enjoins that resolutions can only be adopted, not by two-thirds of those present and voting, but by two-thirds of the entire membership of the O.A.U., whether present or not.

In my opinion the problems of making our Organisation an effective instrument of achieving African aspirations is such a vital matter for the future of the O.A.U. that our Organisation should continue to keep it in view. In addition to the unanimous decision taken that my proposal should be studied by Member States and a report submitted to the next session of the Assembly, I am also giving notice that I will place the question of the setting up of an Executive Council as an amendment to the Charter in accordance with Article 33 of the Charter. Member States of the O.A.U. will be notified in writing accordingly in due course. I hope that at our next meeting it will be possible to determine the functions and responsibilities of such a Council and establish it.

I think that we can take pride in our achievements at this Assembly. We must never forget that the people of Africa demand the utmost from us in our effort to consummate the hopes and aspirations of our continent. I am confident that we will measure up to the expectations of our people as long as we keep before us the guiding principles which have led us and our people individually to achieve independence.

As the Assembly ends its deliberations, I would like to extend to you my brotherly good wishes and those of the Government and people of Ghana for the happiness and prosperity of our various States. I hope that your stay in Ghana has been pleasant and interesting, in spite of the hard work you have done. From all points of view the Conference has been worthwhile. I sincerely hope that there will be another opportunity of having you again with us either individually or collectively. Goodbye, good luck and Godspeed.

22

THE GREAT TASKS AHEAD

1966 NEW YEAR MESSAGE

December 31, 1965

FRIENDS AND COUNTRYMEN,

In a few hours' time a new year, 1966, will be in with us. It is right that on the last day of the old year we should take stock of the year that will soon pass away and consider what we can and ought to do in the year that is about to be born.

As we cast our minds back over events in 1965, we should all be grateful that in spite of the stresses and strains of the past year world peace has been maintained. The crisis in Southern Rhodesia, the cruel war in Vietnam, the unfortunate conflict between India and Pakistan, and the situation in the Dominican Republic all have threatened and still threaten world peace.

As in past years Ghana has played its part peacefully to resolve these conflicts. Over the years we have pursued in concert with other non-aligned nations a policy which has had a number of successes. The idea that Africa should be a nuclear free zone has been reflected in a resolution of the United Nations and by the decision of the Organisation of African Unity. Our pressure for genuine disarmament is increasingly influencing world opinion. We shall continue to press for complete and general disarmament. In particular we must be on our guard against limited wars being used by major powers to secure the political advantages which formerly they sought by general war. For this reason it is international friction of which the present German situation is only one example.

One of the more serious threats to world peace which arose during this year is the present Southern Rhodesian issue about whose danger Ghana had warned the world over and over again in past years. There is no need for further meetings either by the Organisation of African Unity or the Commonwealth on what

136

should be done about Rhodesia. This has already been decided. What is required of us in the coming year is to carry out faithfully decisions already made including the use of force. We should be proud that Ghana was one of the first African States to carry out the Organisation of African Unity Southern Rhodesian decisions.

Looking back over the problems in Africa this year, one issue stands out crystal clear, namely, the need for a Continental Union Government. Everything that has happened in Africa in the year that is closing has demonstrated once again, and beyond any possible shadow of doubt, that unless we are able to form an effective Union Government for our Continent, we shall not only continue to be at the mercy of those forces which profit from our division, but the future of our Continent will be very dark indeed, and may lead into confusion, further errors and even anarchy.

We have good reason to be proud of the progress that has been made this year towards our goal of a United Africa. There is no leader in Africa today who can truthfully say that African Unity, and for that matter a Union Government for Africa, is not feasible. The time is not far distant when the pressure of African mass opinion will force those who now drag their feet to match their words by action. Those who champion African Unity should be encouraged and stimulated even by the vicious attacks which are daily made against them, both outside and inside Africa. So long as we continue to advocate effective and genuine independence for Africa and its political unification, so long shall we be subject to slanderous and mischievous misrepresentation by those who have a vested interest in keeping Africa weak, disunited and balkanised. These are decisive moments in our history where direct intervention of the masses of the people of Africa shall sweep away the reactionary obstructionists and lay the foundation of a new Africa.

One of the mechanisms of neo-colonialism is to hire African traitors and stooges—agents provocateurs—to spread lies and untruths about the progressive States of Africa, and their dedicated leaders. Neo-colonialist errors and contradictions which rend Africa asunder will find their natural solution within the framework of a Continental Union Government for Africa.

If we are to defeat the neo-colonialists in their endeavours, it is necessary to understand the essence of neo-colonialism. The essence of neo-colonialism is that it seeks to use the wealth of the older developed countries to impoverish the developing states. Neo-colonialism would establish a parasitic world in which some ten per cent of the world's population live in luxury on the labours of the other ninety per cent. It is against this system that we fight and not against any particular countries or group of countries or governments, or their leaders as such.

We know that neo-colonialism uses foreign investment as one of its weapons. However, this does not mean that we are against foreign investment as such. What we are against is its misuse and the attempt to use foreign investment to control, direct and manipulate the political and economic future of a developing country.

Two courses are open to those who control the vast financial resources of the developed countries. There is the neo-colonialist course. I have recently pointed out that by pursuing a neo-colonialist policy the monopoly-capitalists of the developed countries are signing their own death warrant. In the long run, neo-colonialism will prove as disastrous to those who practise it as it is now to those who are its victims. It is impossible to conceive that a system can long endure which results in a small fraction of the world's population becoming wealthier and wealthier, while the great majority of mankind become poorer and poorer. It is therefore as much in the interest of the developed countries as of the developing to bring an end to neo-colonialism. This is why I have repeatedly pleaded for an exploration of the alternative course, namely co-operation, upon a new basis, between the developed and the developing countries. As I have often said, developing countries need investment from outside. Such investment could be an important factor in narrowing the ever-growing gap between the 'haves' and the 'have-nots', between the developed countries and the developing countries. Unfortunately, the present direction of much foreign investment serves to widen, and not to narrow, this gaping gap. Ghana's policy is socialist, but we welcome co-operation with all States whether they be capitalist or socialist. We welcome foreign investment, provided only that such investment fits in with our own national plans for development, and helps to increase our economic growth and not to retard it.

We can understand that investment by foreign interests and governments in less developed countries may involve an element of risk for the investor. For instance, there may be a drastic decline in the world price of some export commodities upon which the developing country depends in order to find the foreign exchange to repay the investment in question.

There is enough potential capital and resources in the world today to enable both developed and developing countries to progress, until the present distinction between the developed and developing nations disappears. If there was a politically unimpeded flow of capital we could all build for ourselves a prosperous and contented world. Here, I have a suggestion, in this connection. The developing countries might contribute to and support an international organisation which would provide insurance to foreign investors against any possible risks in investing in any particular developing country which was a party to the scheme. After all, it is only fair that we take into account the point of view of the investor in a developing country. Such an organisation as I have in mind could be established under the aegis of the United Nations. If such an organisation were established, it would be possible for foreign investment to be given to developing countries without any political or other strings whatsoever. The ostensible reason for attaching such strings is often given as the need to protect foreign investment. But such an idea as I am proposing requires further study; notwithstanding, I am convinced it is a feasible and practical method of resolving one of the obstacles to capital investment in developing countries.

Here, I would appeal to the Great Powers to show greater understanding of the problems facing the developing countries. Every country, however great, has to pass through a critical phase of development. By their very existence the developed countries present to the developing countries an image of what the future might be for them. For this reason, developed countries should be careful not to allow political and superprofit considerations to blind them to their obligations to the rest of the world. Irrespective of the political systems we follow, we are all treading the same road to full and better development.

This is why Ghana regrets that the United States Government

139

should recently have attempted to prevent a free dialogue on these matters between us by the publicised declaration to impose food sanctions on Ghana. Since this incident has been given much publicity, let me state the facts. For over a year now, the Government had been negotiating with the United States Government without results for the supply to Ghana of some of the surplus food which they cannot dispose of in the United States. Ghana felt justified in making this request to the United States Government since, as everyone knows, Ghana supplies large quantities of food to the United States in the form of cocoa for which during 1965 a fair price could not be obtained owing to the manipulations of the international market. Our negotiations for the supply of surplus food from America were still proceeding when they were suddenly broken off by the United States Government, apparently on account of my recent book, *Neo-Colonialism: The Last Stage of Imperialism.*

It is clear that food so heavily laden with strings could prove indigestible in Ghana. Nevertheless, I would like to take this opportunity to assure our many friends and well-wishers in the United States that this unhappy and, I trust, isolated incident will in no way be allowed to impair the long-standing friendly and cordial relations between Ghana and the people and Government of the United States. Indeed, our great Volta Dam at Akosombo and the gigantic Aluminium Smelter being built at Tema provide evidence of the friendly and mutually useful co-operation which exists between Ghana and the United States.

January, 1966, will see the official opening of the Volta Dam Project. Ghana is already producing from the Dam electrical power at a cost which can compete favourably with any in the world. This Dam and its Lake, the largest man-made lake in the world, are proof that we have wisely used our resources and that true co-operation benefits both sides.

We are on the road to progress, and there is no time for complacency or easy optimism. We are grateful to those friendly countries and organisations who are helping us along this road. But let us realise that if we are to achieve our national goals and aspirations, it will be in the main through our own united and sustained efforts for progress, freedom and prosperity. We are a young and vigorous nation and there is nothing we cannot achieve if we remain united, vigilant and true to our cause.

Within the last few years our industrialisation programme has been making great progress. Already, made-in-Ghana products like our beer, corned beef, chocolates, cocoa bags, glassware, aluminium household products, and building materials, such as cement, paint and aluminium sheets, etc. etc., are being put on the market as quickly as our resources permit. Very soon our gold refinery at Tarkwa will be in production and we shall be in full control of our gold resources. I must, therefore, call on the Ministries, State Corporations and organisations to carry out their duties with increased devotion, efficiency and honesty, and with respect and concern for our State property. This call goes to all the other public services and State organs. Happily, we have a Civil Service which is one of the best in the world. It is vigorous, loyal and incorruptible.

So, at this time, all sections of our community, our churches, voluntary organisations, market women's organisations, workers, farmers and peasants, must mobilise their energies and resources—physical, mental, moral and spiritual—for the great tasks that lie ahead of us all.

I know, and I am confident, that in this spirit of dedication and resolve, in this spirit of confident in ourselves, we shall win even greater victories and successes in the coming year.

I wish you all, wherever you may be, health and happiness in this New Year.

Good Night, and God bless you all.

Printed in the United States
76764LV00005B/293